THE TEACHING OF POETRY
European Perspectives

Also available from Cassell:

E. Bearne (ed.): *Greater Expectations: Children Reading Writing*
E. Bearne, M. Styles and V. Watson: *The Prose and the Passion: Children and their Reading*
J. Britton: *Literature in its Place*
C. Fox: *At the Very Edge of the Forest*
L. Hall: *An Anthology of Poetry by Women*
L. Hall: *Poetry for Life*
G. Heard: *For the Good of Earth and Sun: Teaching Poetry*
A. Stables: *An Approach to English*
M. Styles, E. Bearne and V. Watson: *After Alice: Exploring Children's Literature*
S. Tchudi and S. Tchudi: *The English Language Arts Handbook*
K. Topping: *Paired Reading, Writing and Spelling*
G. West: *An Approach to Shakespeare*

The Teaching of Poetry

European Perspectives

Edited by
Linda Thompson

CASSELL

Cassell
Wellington House
125 Strand
London WC2R 0BB

215 Park Avenue South
New York
NY 10003

© Linda Thompson and the contributors, 1996

All rights reserved. No part of this publication may be
reproduced or transmitted in any form or by any means,
electronic or mechanical including photocopying, recording
or any information storage or retrieval system, without
prior permission in writing from the publishers.

First published 1996

British Library Cataloguing-in-Publication Data
A catalogue record for this book is available from the British Library.

Library of Congress Cataloging-in-Publication Data
The teaching of poetry: European perspectives / edited by Linda
  Thompson.
    p. cm.
    Includes bibliographical references and index.
    ISBN 0-304-32876-6 (hard). — ISBN 0-304-32878-2 (pbk.)
    1. Poetry — Study and teaching — Europe.   I. Thompson, Linda.
PN1101.T39 1996
808.1'07'04 — dc20   95-40563
                                                                       CIP

ISBN 0-304-32876-6 (hardback)
     0-304-32878-2 (paperback)

Typeset by Chapter One (London)
Printed and bound in Great Britain by Redwood Books, Trowbridge, Wiltshire

Contents

The Contributors		vii
Preface		xi
Acknowledgements		xiv
1	Trees and Stuff: Young Children's Constructs of Poetry *Linda Thompson*	1
2	Poetry as Play: Rules for the Imagination *Gundel Mattenklott*	12
3	Reading Poetry and Primary School Practice *Linda Hall*	22
4	Ways of Experiencing Poetry and Acquiring Poetic Knowledge in Secondary School *Thorkild Borup Jensen*	30
5	Poetry Teaching in the Secondary School: The Concept of 'Difficulty' *Mike Fleming*	37
6	Creative Writing in Foreign Language Teaching *Carol Morgan*	44
7	Teaching Poetry in the Secondary School in France *Jean-Marie Fournier*	55
8	Teaching of Poetry in the Netherlands since 1968 *Willem de Moor*	63
9	Thinking Through Form: Preparing to Teach Poetry in School *Colin Walter*	77
10	Making Sense of Poetry: Beginning Teachers Talking about Poems *Peter Millward*	85
Name Index		95
Subject Index		97

The Contributors

Willem de Moor is Associate Professor and Head of the Literary Education Department at the Faculty of Letters, Catholic University in Nijmegen, The Netherlands. He has extensive experience of teaching in secondary schools and teacher education. He has written several books including literary criticism and biographies.

Mike Fleming is Director of the PGCE secondary course at the University of Durham. He has been a deputy headteacher in a comprehensive school and is co-author of *Ways of Feeling*, a textbook for secondary school pupils. His academic writing includes *Pupils' Perceptions of the Nature of Poetry* (1992).

Jean-Marie Fournier is a researcher at the Institut National de Recherche Pedagogique (INRP), Paris, France. He has conducted a number of large-scale research projects in the field of education.

Linda Hall is a Senior Lecturer in English at Trinity College, Carmarthen. She has taught in a variety of primary and secondary schools in Inner London. She has published articles on poetry as well as other aspects of primary and secondary practice in professional journals, including *Junior Education* and *The Times Educational Supplement*. *Poetry For Life: A Practical Guide to Teaching Poetry in the Primary School* was published in 1989 by Cassell; her second book, *An Anthology of Women Poets* for GCSE/A level, is also published by Cassell.

Thorkild Borup Jensen is Assistant Professor of Danish Literature at the Royal Danish School of Educational Studies, Copenhagen. He has written a number of books including *Introduction to Drama*, *From Book to Screen*, *Pedagogy of Literature* and *A History of the Danish Identity*.

Gundel Mattenklott is Professor at Hochshule der Künste in Berlin. Her books include *Literaische Geselligkeit* (1979); *KinderMachen Theater* (1983) and *Kinderliteratur seit 1945* (1989).

Peter Millward is Director of the BA (Ed) degree at the University of Durham, and was formerly a deputy headteacher of a primary school. His research interests include the teaching of drama and poetry. He has written *Drama as a Well Made Play* (1990) and *Children Talking About Poetry* (1994) with Linda Thompson.

Carol Morgan is the Modern Languages Tutor on the PGCE secondary course at the University of Bath. She has previously worked as a Senior Research Assistant at the University of Durham on a project investigating the cultural awareness dimension in the French A-level syllabus. She has taught German, French, EFL and English literature at schools and universities in England, France and Germany.

Linda Thompson is a Senior Lecturer in Education at the University of Durham. She has taught in nursery and infant schools in Britain and at universities in the Netherlands and Sweden. She has co-edited *Language and Culture* (1992) and has written a number of articles on early years education and young bilingual children.

Colin Walter was formerly Lecturer in Education at Goldsmiths' College, University of London. He has written extensively on the teaching and learning of poetry. His publications include *Inhibiting Poetry* (1989) and *BP Teachers' Resource File for Poetry* (1992). He is currently Honorary Research Associate, University of Greenwich.

The genesis of language is not to be found in the prosaic but in the poetic side of life.

Otto Jesperson, 1921

Preface

Traditionally the curriculum has been divided, some might say artificially, into the teaching of language on the one hand, and the teaching of literature on the other. The teaching of poetry has conventionally fallen on the literature side of this divide. This volume attempts to build bridges across and between various sub-divisions within the language curriculum.

In September 1992 colleagues in the Language in Education Research Group (Mike Fleming, Peter Millward and Linda Thompson) at the School of Education, University of Durham, hosted a symposium on the teaching of poetry. The symposium was attended by teachers and researchers from a number of European institutions who presented papers reflecting their current thinking on the teaching of poetry in a variety of contexts. The papers from the Durham Poetry Symposium are collected together in this volume; they present the case for teaching poetry as both literature and language, and argue for a place for the teaching of poetry in the teaching of all languages. The ideas emanate from an eclectic group of established researchers in a number of European countries (Denmark, England, France, Germany, The Netherlands and Wales). All are currently involved in teaching poetry to a wide range of pupils. The papers draw together a rich and diverse range of suggestions for teaching poetry at all ages from the infant school through to students in teacher education courses. We believe this collection to be unique: researchers together explore the implications of their work for educating teachers and teaching poetry in the classroom.

Sadly, there is one aspect on which we all agree: poetry is a frequently neglected aspect of the language curriculum. This volume explores the reasons for this and suggests ideas to enable non-specialist teachers to enliven current practice, together with research findings to illuminate national and international discussions about the role and status of poetry in the curriculum. The ideas and suggestions are drawn from a range of European contexts. We hope they will inform teachers of all languages in a range of teaching situations. Above all we hope that they will help to restore teachers' professional confidence in teaching poetry and so nurture more positive attitudes towards poetry among teachers and pupils.

Special thanks and acknowledgements are due to our colleague Professor Mike Byram who helped us to realize this symposium, and to the support received from the School of Education Research Committee.

The book is divided informally into three sections. The first section addresses poetry in the primary school. The section begins with a report on the Durham Poetry Project, 'Trees and Stuff: Young Children's Constructs of Poetry', which presents the findings of an ethnographic study of the ideas that young children hold about poetry and the language they use when talking about it to their peers and their teachers. The starting point for the second chapter, Gundel Mattenklott's 'Poetry as Play: Rules for the Imagination', is the inherent enjoyment children have for games and playing. She links this with the seemingly infinite capacity of children (and adults) for creativity. In considering poetry as play she places emphasis on extending activities that are already known and enjoyed into the teaching of poetry. She describes a number of activities which she has used successfully for teaching poetry to primary school children and their teachers. The activities address the teaching of formal aspects such as rhyme and metaphor as well as less common aspects of poetry. Her activities emphasize an interdisciplinary approach to poetry teaching. She combines art, music and drama with poetry to stimulate classroom activities. In the third and final chapter in this section Linda Hall addresses the very important topic of 'Reading Poetry and Primary School Practice'. She echoes the recurrent theme of poetry as a much neglected aspect of the school curriculum. However, she goes beyond this and suggests that even where it does exist it frequently is as a functional inclusion in topic work, detracting from the poems' intrinsic qualities and humane values. She argues that these methods and approaches distort and damage the value and nature of poetry. She acknowledges the central place accorded to reading in primary classrooms and suggests that poetry could be included in private, individual reading sessions that are currently a feature of so many primary classrooms. This would allow children the opportunity to reflect on the poem, their reading of it, and on associated ideas and experiences drawn from their own lives. She suggests that poetry may be the most enjoyable way to teach phonics and to develop children's phonemic awareness, a key feature in learning to read.

The second section addresses poetry in the secondary school years. This section begins with Thorkild Borup Jensen's account from Denmark of 'Ways of Experiencing Poetry and Acquiring Poetic Knowledge in Secondary School'. This chapter identifies a number of practical ways in which teachers and pupils can together experience poetry, ways that address knowledge about poetic language. Although the ideas are based on work in secondary classrooms, the suggestions also provide a useful starting point for the non-specialist teacher at Key Stage 2 in primary schools.

In the chapter 'Poetry Teaching in the Secondary School: The Concept of "Difficulty"' Mike Fleming explores the commonly held perception of poetry as an area of the English curriculum that pupils find difficult. He suggests that in order to overcome pupils' initial reluctance to read poetry the curriculum can be expanded to include a broader range of poetry, including jingles, song lyrics and rapping. In this way it is hoped that pupils' attitudes to the genre will gradually begin to change.

Carol Morgan continues this section with her presention of a number of practical classroom activities for introducing poetry writing to secondary school children. Based on her experience of teaching French and German to secondary school pupils in Britain, and English to speakers of other languages, she explains a range of strategies that she has found successful for motivating foreign-language learners. She combines sound classroom practice with underpinning rationale for the activities she describes. Drawing on an established body of literature she presents a cogent argument for a place for creative writing in foreign-language classrooms, irrespective of the language being taught.

'Teaching Poetry in the Secondary School in France' is a report by Jean-Marie Fournier on a large-scale study carried out by a team of researchers at the French National Institute of Pedagogical Research in Paris (INRP). The study provides a comprehensive overview of the range of texts that students study for the oral element of the French Literature *baccalauréat* examination (the examination taken at the end of secondary school education in France). Analysis of the corpus demonstrates trends in the type and range of texts studied by students in secondary schools across France. This national overview provides a useful insight for French educators. It is interesting to note the consistency in both the types of texts and the domination of particular texts selected for study in an education system where teachers have free choice over the content of their lessons. This suggests that a uniformity in curriculum content emerges without a national curriculum or government legislation. Findings from the survey suggest that poems are frequently selected because they are representative of a particular literary trend or style rather than for their inherent literary qualities.

In Chapter 8 Willem de Moor draws on his experience of teaching in the USA and the Netherlands to outline a model of teaching poetry that combines what he refers to as a 'text-studying approach' with ways of 'text-experiencing'. He uses the poem 'Melopee' by the Flemish poet Paul van Ostaijen , to exemplify the approach. His view is that once the poet has published the poem (the poet's text) it is then left to the readers to read and re-read the poem and to arrive at their own understanding and interpretation of the poem. This is what de Moor calls 'the reader's text'. In the classroom this means that the teacher and the pupil may all arrive at individual interpretations of the poem. He describes collaborative ways of teaching including group work, using tape-recorders and drawings that allow the pupils' texts to lead the discussion and interpretation of the poem. His view is that it is only when pupils have constructed texts of their own do they become curious to know more about the poet's own text, the original poem.

Section three is concerned with the possibilities for poetry in teacher education. Colin Walter, in his chapter 'Thinking Through Form: Preparing to Teach Poetry in School', outlines specific suggestions for the teaching of poetry in classrooms, together with the work of those who have influenced his thinking, including Vygotsky, Geertz and Jakobson. He presents the view that language is of the nature of poetry. Quoting Brodsky he argues that poetry is not mere entertainment or art, it is our anthropological, genetic goal without which we can only be sublingual. He outlines an approach to the teaching of poetry in the primary school in which he emphasizes the symbiosis between listeners, readers, tellers and composers of poetic texts in public and private contexts where intertextuality is developed within the company of others. His advocated approach places particular emphasis upon the ontogenetic nature of child language development. His claim is that the earliest encouragement of poetry is best nurtured concurrently with an interest in reading, writing and sharing with others. The approach outlined and the suggestions for classroom activities described are suitable for a wide variety of learners from primary school pupils of all ages to students on initial teacher-education courses. Poetry is not a goal that we as teachers should aim for, it is where we should begin.

Our collection ends with Peter Millward's description of the perceptions of poetry shared by a group of beginning teachers. Chapter 10, 'Making Sense of Poetry', describes the language used by a group of PGCE Primary students when they talk about poems. The chapter describes the ways in which the students, who are training to be primary school teachers, reveal their understanding of poetry through group interaction. It is suggested that although responses to poetry are essentially personalized, people arrive at a better understanding of their own ideas when they talk to others. There is clear evidence here that newly qualified teachers do have clear perceptions of poetry. This augurs well for the future of poetry teaching in our schools, colleges and universities.

Linda Thompson
University of Durham

Acknowledgements

Chapter 4. 'Widescreen' by Benny Andersen. Reprinted by permission of the publishers from *Selected Poems* (translated by Alexander Taylor). Published by Princeton University Press © 1975.

Chapter 4. 'Poem 657' by Emily Dickinson. Reprinted by permission of the publishers and the Trustees of Amherst College from *The Poems of Emily Dickinson* (edited by Thomas H. Johnson). Cambridge, MA: The Belknap Press of Harvard University Press. © 1951, 1955, 1979, 1983 by the President and Fellows of Harvard College.

Chapter 5. 'This is just to say' by William Carlos Williams. Reprinted by permission of the publishers from *Collected Poems 1909–1939*, vol. 1. Published in America by New Directions Publishing Company and in the UK by Carcanet Press © 1987.

Chapter 1

Trees and Stuff:
Young Children's Constructs of Poetry

Linda Thompson

> *In the Emperor's court, a flow of poetry has begun,*
> *Keep, O God, the door of this treasure of pearls open.*
> Ghalib

INTRODUCTION

This collection begins with a chapter that presents the findings of a research project carried out in primary schools in the north-east of England. It poses the questions: What constructs of poetic genre have been formed by children at the ages of six and ten years and what metalanguage do they have for talking about these constructs?

1988 saw the introduction of two important influences in the education of young children in the UK: the Education Reform Act, which introduced English as a core subject for all children in compulsory education, and the Kingman Report, which recommended that all teachers and pupils should have a knowledge of how the English language works (KAL). Both were introduced into the primary school curriculum on the unfounded assumption that their inclusion would ameliorate standards of literacy. The project presented here was planned with a view to finding out what young children already know about language form and function, as a prerequisite to planning an appropriate curriculum for English which includes an element of KAL teaching.

Poetry was chosen as a suitable focus for a number of reasons. It had already been identified by HMI (1988) and other professional sources (DES, 1982) as a neglected element of the English curriculum. It was also perceived by pupils and teachers alike as 'difficult' (Touponce, 1990). Previous approaches to the teaching of poetry in schools have included literary appreciation (e.g. Levin, 1962), which focuses on isolated features of the genre (e.g. metaphor, simile) as a 'marked' use of language, deviant rather than specific. In contrast, the aesthetic-response approach focuses on the appreciation of content (e.g. Benton *et al*, 1988) but frequently neglects the linguistic features of the genre. Post-1988 both of these approaches seem inadequate. Yet the unfounded assertions of Kingman deserve closer scrutiny. Hence it was felt that the unique form and specific linguistic features of the poetic genre, together with its relative neglect in the school curriculum, rendered it suitable for exploring children's untutored or intuitive knowledge of language use.

METHODOLOGY

Data was collected from a number of different classrooms (Year 2 and Year 6) in different schools. Discourse data representing two different styles of speech was collected from child informants aged six and ten years and their teachers: vernacular (casual child–child) speech and more formal (pupil–teacher) interactions. This data was collected in the form of candid audio-tape recordings while the children were engaged in separate but related activities. First, in small groups of three or four, the informants were asked to sort a number of texts. This activity yielded the vernacular data. Then they were asked to report their decisions to the teacher. This provided the sample of more formal talk.

Carter and Nash (1990) have identified a number of stylistic features that distinguish poetry (poetic structures) from other forms of writing. These include:

- the way poets pattern language to produce specific effects
- the phonaesthetic contouring (patterns of sound)
- the organization and patterning of the text
- the creation of text-intensive poetic meaning
- the stylistic contrasts (grammatical, syntactical, lexical)
- the use of modality
- the clause structure
- the isomorphic fit between language structure and meaning.

Using these features as a framework, it is evident from the analysis of the data that children share the perceptions, if not the terminology, of these characteristic features of poetry.

CHILDREN'S PERCEPTIONS OF POETIC FORM

Carter and Nash (1990: 115) describe poetry as the creation of text-intensive meaning through the organization and patterning of a text. From the data it is apparent that pupils are familiar with this idea of the patterning of the genre. Their recognition of patterning falls into three types: the acknowledgement of the poet's deliberate contouring of the language; the visual impact of the finished poem; and the influence that this quality asserts on the reader. There is evidence in the data to suggest that pupils are aware of all of these aspects of form, both in the poems that they have written themselves and in those which others have written. The following examples are from pupils talking about their personal experience of the writing process. They demonstrate an awareness of the need to organize and pattern text for the genre and an appreciation of the effort involved in attempting to do this:

> In poems you have to make it fit … not just any way … you have to try and make it.

There is also recognition of the writer's task:

> At the beginning I just put down the first idea … just keep on putting down ideas and gradually get more ideas. I put them all down. Sometimes they have to be rearranged better.

There is similar recognition of other poets' efforts to sculpt and hone the language during the writing process. In response to the question 'What would you look for were you to judge a poetry competition?' the following comments were made:

> A poem that flowed and didn't have too many statements ... one that had quite a few facts but not written down in facts like.

Pupils thus demonstrated an awareness of the deliberate contouring of language that characterizes poetry. There is evidence in the corpus to suggest that this awareness exists amongst children as young as six years. Their experience of writing poetry is naturally more limited, so they do not draw on their own experiences in the same way to illustrate their perceptions. Instead they draw attention to the visual impact made by a poem as a result of the deliberate contouring of the language. The following comment serves to illustrate this:

> It looks like a rhyme ... it's more like a poem.

There is also a sense in which the visual feature becomes the deciding factor as to whether or not a particular text belongs to the genre of poetry, as demonstrated by the pupil who said:

> When you read it it doesn't make sense ... it's only when you see it.

When faced with a text that was not actually a poem, the visual impact was similarly seen to make an impression:

> I still think this looks rhymish ... yeah ... I think that rhymes.

Some pupils demonstrate a more developed sense of poetic form and link it with other distinguishing features of the genre. The following comment illustrates an awareness of the different set of demands that poetry writing makes on a writer in comparison with those made on others writing in different literary genres:

> I think writing poems is hard because stories like you can write anything you can write about anything but in poems you have to make it and not just any way you have to try and make it as though you could say it like a poem.

There is also evidence here that the pupil was aware of the strong aural quality of poetry (a feature that will be discussed in detail in the next section).

Recognition of this aural quality is echoed in another comment from a different pupil who was more specific about the nature of the aural features of poems. In reflecting on his own experience of writing poetry, this pupil acknowledged the necessity for deliberate contouring of the language to achieve the desired outcome. However, he went beyond this to identify other aspects of text-contouring in the form of rhyme and lexical choice.

> It is hard to think of words that will actually go with them that rhyme ... you have to think of words that will go together in a poem that will sound right ... you have to think of words that will rhyme ... they don't have to rhyme at all.

This brings us to a second category of poetic form as identified by the pupils, namely the aural quality of the genre.

THE AURAL QUALITY

In any composition of a literary kind, we assume the presence of the spoken word in the written. The aesthetic attributes of speech sounds are most intensively exploited in poetry (Carter and Nash, 1990: 119). Poets usually pattern language to produce specific sound effects and this is frequently recognized by pupils. The following example shows that the pupil recognizes the importance of this aural quality:

> Bits sound like a poem ... 'The Bishop chanting grace' sounds more like a poem than anything else.

This strong sense of the aural quality as a feature of the poetic genre is also shown in the following quotes where pupils demonstrate an awareness of the spoken word in the written form of the poem:

> What makes me think it is a kind of a poem is the way she said it ... like it's more like a song.
>
> I usually say poems like that [demonstration] and stories another way.
>
> Helen said it more like a poem.

From these examples it is clear that some pupils are able to recognize that it is the reading aloud which makes the density of the sound effects more apparent, both to the reciter and the listener. Pupils also recognize that this phonic quality of text-density is the outcome of the deliberate organization and patterning.

Rhyme

Some pupils identify this aural quality more specifically as rhyme. Rhyme has been identified as a strong general identifying feature of the genre:

> Poems rhyme and that can be.
>
> I like it because it rhymes and I like things that rhyme.

Other pupils selected specific rhyming lexical items from a text, in support of their decision to call particular texts poems:

> This rhymes ... rye and pie ... I'll put that in the poem box ... sing and king ... honey and money ... blackbird ... nose ... no ... clothes nose.
>
> We think it's a rhyme in a way; ate rhymes with grace and it repeats ate three times. It's more like a poem.

Rhyme has been identified as a feature of the genre even when individual pupils have not used the appropriate metalanguage to talk about it:

> That's a poem ... I think it's more a poem ... tucket bucket ... queen queen.

While rhyme was often selected by pupils as an identifying feature of the genre, some pupils also recognized the limitations of the rhyme format, particularly when used in their own writing of poems:

> If I do two lines that rhyme I usually try to make them not rhyme ... it doesn't sound very good but it's a sort of habit ... it's not deliberately rhyming ... it doesn't sound very good if it's a rhyming bit.

It was acknowledged that rhyme is only one possible form for a poem to take:

> Poems doesn't always have to rhyme.

Rhyme, then, was identified by pupils, by both name and examples, as an identifying feature of poetry.

Rhythm

The general rhythmic organization of poems was identified by pupils as another aspect of the aural quality of the genre:

> When I read poems and they are new I just make up a sort of tune to go along with them.

This was seen as a distinctive feature of poetry in comparison with other genres:

> A story is more like writing ... it doesn't even sound like it could get a tune to it ... and in other ways a poem does make tunes on it and some of them don't ... most poems have tunes ... most poems have a little rhyme of their own.

The fact that this rhythmic organization is achieved in part through the device of repetition was evident to the pupils, who were not always convinced of the effects produced:

> He uses gallop too much ... we like this but he [*the poet*] uses gallop a lot ... there's a gallop ... there's a gallop ... there's a gallop ... there's a gallop ... there's a gallop.

> Well, in the first verse it says 'man' a bit too much and I don't like it when they rhyme with the same words.

These pupils are articulating not only their recognition of the stylistic poetic feature of repetition but also a developing critical faculty for the genre.

It can be seen from the evidence presented that pupils demonstrate an awareness of the aural qualities of poetry in a number of ways. They acknowledge the strong link between the written poem and the way it would sound if recited. Recitation is considered to be an appropriate rendering of a poem, as demonstrated in this remark:

> You can memorize the poems and sometimes the stories but I think poems are much better.

Pupils talking about poetry are aware that poets organize and pattern the language to produce specific sound effects which serve as a stylistic signpost to the genre. Carter and Nash (1990: 115) refer to this technique as 'the ... phonaesthetic contouring of patterns of sound'. Children talking about poetry frequently make reference to this feature, as has been demonstrated in the range of pupil comments already presented.

The theme of lexical appropriateness was echoed in another interview when pupils were talking about the poems they had written:

> I couldn't put dead ... it wouldn't look right.

> You have to think of some words and see if they fit ... if you use not long words ... that makes it sound too factual ... if you use words that seem to fit you know all the time what makes it good.

> If that was a rhyme they'd probably say morn instead of morning ... if I was making that a rhyme I'd put morn instead of morning.

There was also an element of critical awareness of the poetry written by peers:

> But not too many (long words) ... Stuart uses too many long words and makes it sound silly ... he uses dead long words.

They recognized that the function of this phonetic component is primarily aesthetic and is an aspect of the organizational patterning which makes the genre unique:

> If it was just a story you wouldn't say 'tulips, tulips' you would say 'tulips' ... because a story is nothing like this.

Whether or not pupils share Carter and Nash's (1990) recognition of the other functions of language contouring such as acoustic punctuation or as a designator of boundaries requires further clarification. This can only be fully explored in a detailed analysis of the corpus with respect to this single aspect. Pupils do, however, recognize the potential of the genre for introducing them to new aspects of language use and this is viewed as positive:

> It had lots of different words in it ... and ones you'd never heard before ... I'm really positive ... it's a really nice poem.

Pupils are also clear that syntax has a role to play in the patterning of poetic genre. In their talk pupils illustrate an awareness of the deliberateness with which poetic form is styled. Although they do not draw a distinction between the lexical and syntactical choices made by poets, they are aware of the two as different, as they demonstrate in the samples of text that they select to illustrate their discussions about the genre. This is apparent when pupils talk about what they would look for if they were to judge a poetry competition:

> A poem that flowed and did not have too many statements in it ... one that had quite a few facts but not written down in facts like the church has tall pinnacles because that's not very good ... more like church with its tall pinnacles.

> It would be too long a line if I put this church is a never-ending life ... if you put it in a whole line you would have to use something like is because you couldn't put this church is a never ending life on one line ... that's all right because one sentence isn't saying this is when it's saying something lingers there ... one statement not like that ... it usually just flows.

Pupils frequently show that they have a developed sense of syntactical appropriateness:

> If I just read that bit it tells me that it definitely is a poem ... colours red, yellow and black because I wouldn't put that in a story.

If pupils' expectations of the syntax of the genre are not met, they then begin to question their categorization of a particular text as a poem. This pupil was talking about a text that was not actually a poem but which contained many features that could be accurately accredited to the genre:

> I think this one ['Chloe and Maude'] is like a poem ... but I still don't know why it starts with 'so'.

These examples demonstrate an awareness of the syntactical patterning even when pupils make no explicit reference to it. This awareness extended to the children's own writing of poetry:

> The title just sort of comes ... I don't know how I think about line-length and titles.

Although the metalanguage is of particular interest, to complete the picture emerging from the data of pupils' developing constructs of poetic genre, there are two further features which it is possible for us to identify: the affective element and the relationship of poetry to other known genres.

THE AFFECTIVE ELEMENT

The affective element has been identified by Carter and Nash (1990:150) as the expression of a creative impulse. This emotive element is identified by pupils when they are talking about what makes a good poem. These are two comments from the same pupil:

> I suppose a poem must have your own feelings in ... I just try and picture it in my mind.

There is also a strong feeling that some topics are particularly well suited to the poetic form. Like this comment (which I've used for the title of this chapter):

> Poetry is about trees and stuff

and from another child,

> Love.

Despite evidence from the data to support the view that pupils do share some of the perceptions of literary critics, this is not the total picture. The corpus contains data which does not fall within these categories and descriptions. Yet it is evident from a number of statements made by the children when they refer to their previous experiences of poetry in the form of nursery rhymes or songs. This category is most prevalent among the younger children and, since it is characterized by its heavy dependence upon previous learning experiences that cannot be identified as specific in time, place or content, it will be referred to as *given or intuitive knowledge*. It signifies the tacit acceptance of the existence of poetry in the world.

Characteristic of this category is the recall of a number of familiar nursery rhymes that represents learning which has taken place but has been subsequently forgotten. The examples may or may not have been overtly taught. This is taken to be evidence of given or intuitive knowledge (which is different from, and not to be confused with, an innate predisposition to language learning). The recall of intuitive knowledge is almost second nature. The pupils can raise this knowledge unconsciously. It is commonplace, effortless recall. In conversation with others, pupils used a metalanguage – rhyme, poem, nursery rhymes – as an elliptic referent to their given knowledge and took for granted that their interlocutors shared this tacit knowledge. It was frequently presented as a statement of fact, as can be seen in the following extracts:

> There is a Miss Muffett so we reckoned that [Little Miss Tucket] might be a nursery rhyme too ... and we know that's [Sing a Song of Sixpence] a nursery rhyme.

There is evidence that it is not only poetry that has a place in this category. Children share a similar conviction when talking about other genres:

> I know ... they're songs.

> And we know that's a letter because you said it started with dear and that's the way letters start.

> That's a sort of skipping rhyme, do you have any skipping rhymes? There's one I got out of a reading book on Lilian the Vacuum Cleaner, it's a skipping rhyme ... in the kitchen skipping along, along came a tiger and pushed me out ... something like that.

Pupils demonstrated positively their conviction and certainty of what constitutes a sample text from a particular genre type. There is also evidence to demonstrate an equal conviction about excluding a sample text from a genre type. The following comment was made by a pupil during the text-sorting activity.

> Definitely not a poem.

No further elaboration of this statement was offered. It was presented as self-evident that the sample text did not match the unstated criteria that the pupil was operating in the selection process.

It is the instant, effortless recall that characterizes given knowledge as intuitive knowledge, that is, learning which has taken place but where the circumstances and context of that learning are no longer remembered. In common with all learning, it is dependent for its meaning and value upon the culture in which it was learned. Knowledge of poetic genre as demonstrated by the informants is recognized as culture-bound and context-dependent.

There is also evidence that individuals recall previous experiences of specific texts and use this in making their judgements about text-types. These two pupils illustrate this approach:

> We've heard them before ... we were picking poems and we saw 'Little Miss Tucket' and we already know that 'Sing a Song of Sixpence' is a ... um ... a song ... I mean a poem

> That's a story 'cos I've readed half of it.

In presenting the initial activities to the pupils, the researchers deliberately avoided naming genre types. Despite this, pupils as young as six used the metalanguage of genre types: rhyme, song, nursery rhyme, letter, poem and poetry. Those types identified by the pupils therefore represent their unsolicited recognition of texts and genre types, demonstrating an awareness of poetic and related genres in their linguistic biography and the command in their linguistic repertoire of an accompanying metalanguage for identifying them. Pupils frequently displayed this awareness in this category of given knowledge. It was found to be a feature of the talk of both Year 2 and Year 6 pupils.

THE PROCESS OF ELIMINATION

Moving on from the category of given knowledge, the informants used their previous learning in their attempt to make sense of the new situation with which they were faced. Through a process of elimination they divided the texts into two sets: those which they claimed to know as songs, rhymes or nursery rhymes; and those which they did not recognize as sharing common features with those groups. When the category of given knowledge was exhausted, pupils brought to the fore their knowledge and experience of other genres. Using this information, they went through a process of eliminating texts from the genre-types already known to them as intuitive or given knowledge. This categorization was based on a judgement of the characteristic features not present in a particular text, rather than genre-specific features. By making decisions about which texts were to be excluded from a particular genre-type, pupils were making their judgements on the basis of characteristic features which are absent from the text(s) under scrutiny. They were making decisions about what the texts are not. Examples of this include:

> It's not quite like a story.
>
> A story is nothing like this.

This process is similar to those in more general descriptions of the learning process, when individuals move from the known to the unknown via a new situation or experience.

Thus it can be seen that pupils use a variety of strategies for displaying their constructs of poetic genre. Some quote extracts from texts to illustrate their understanding; others draw on their developing linguistic repertoire and use of a metalanguage, some of which may be poetry-specific and part of which may be borrowed from other literary genres for the purpose of talking about poetry. Their use of the metalanguage, specific or borrowed, may or may not be commensurate with the standard adult use. However, these strategies provide insights into the developing constructs of the genre which pupils have at the ages of six and ten years. They also provide evidence of a developing linguistic repertoire that contains metalanguage for talking about literary genres, one of which is poetry.

TENTATIVE INTERPRETATIONS

The Kingman Report (DES, 1988) proposed that teachers and pupils be explicitly taught about how the English language works – its form, structure and meaning as well as its historical and geographical roots. To be able to talk about the language in this way requires a command of the appropriate metalanguage. However, it is necessary to make a distinction between an individual's ability to recognize specific aspects of language and linguistic form and an ability to talk about them. For the latter, an active command of metalanguage is required. However, the lack of the standard metalanguage in an individual's linguistic repertoire is not necessarily indicative of lack of awareness of the structure of the language in relation to its meaning. In the data presented here it is clear that in the absence of an appropriate metalanguage, children attempt compensatory strategies to communicate their ideas. Without the appropriate metalanguage to talk about poetry, the children attempt to demonstrate their knowledge of the form and structure of the genre in a number of ways. They demonstrate their knowledge by drawing attention to specific features of the text that they regard as genre-specific.

When metalanguage is used, it is sometimes an idiosyncratic use, as demonstrated in this unique comment which defies interpretation:

> Oh, is it like doing a teacher as a simile to a puss moth caterpillar.

A DEVELOPING AWARENESS OF POETIC GENRE: TOWARDS A DESCRIPTIVE FRAMEWORK

The evidence to date suggests that there is a developing awareness of poetic genre amongst children as young as six years and that this awareness of specific features is not always accompanied by the standard metalanguage. The data also suggests that there is a range of genre-specific metalanguage in the linguistic repertoire of children aged between six and ten years but that use of the metalanguage does not always necessarily demonstrate an understanding or appreciation of the specific features to which that metalanguage refers.

From this study it is possible to suggest a proposed framework for genre awareness that seems to be developmental and age-related.

The emerging categories of development are:

1. An appropriate use of the metalanguage for genres as an elliptic referent to the global classification of a text held as common knowledge. These genres include stories, nursery rhymes, songs, as well as poems.
2. The recognition of the genre but without reference to the specific linguistic features of a text.
3. The recognition of the genre on the basis of specific features known to be associated with the genre but absent from the particular text under discussion.
4. The recognition of the genre by reference to its specific features (aural, form, topic etc.) but without use of the appropriate metalanguage.
5. Discussion of the genre with inappropriate use of the metalanguage.

It is suggested that the categories of development outlined here are consistent with a broad framework of developing linguistic knowledge which at Category 1 coincides with an intuitive knowledge of the language in use and which develops through to Category 5 to demonstrate an emergent use of the genre-specific metalanguage (in this case, poetry). It is possible to speculate about the existence of a sixth category that would be defined as the appropriate use of the genre-specific metalanguage. In terms of the development of genre awareness, in this category children would be able to demonstrate the metalanguage of the genre and use it for specific-feature analysis of given texts. It is anticipated that this category would occur at a later stage.

OBSERVATIONS AND INSIGHTS

On the basis of this analysis it is tentatively suggested that children as young as 6 are able to demonstrate an intuitive knowledge of poetic genre and to distinguish between texts that are poems and those which are not. Further, children aged 10 are able to demonstrate the ability to talk about poetic genre and to display a more developed construct of the genre. However, to date the data suggests that children aged 6 and 10 have only a partially developed metalanguage in their linguistic repertoire for talking about poetry.

The findings of this study have implications for the content and organization of the English curriculum for young learners. It is a question of pedagogy. Should the metalanguage be taught to assist with the conceptualization of existing knowledge or should it be taught because it would help to demonstrate existing knowledge to others? Linguistics can only help to answer part of this question. The full answer lies within a philosophy of learning and a pedagogy of education.

ACKNOWLEDGEMENTS

This project was supported by the University of Durham, Research Committee; my colleague Dr Peter Millward, who provided camaraderie and good humour; and the children and teachers who provided the opportunities for me to collect the data. My warm thanks to them all.

REFERENCES

Benton, M., Teasey, J., Bell, R. and Hurst, K. (1988) *Young Readers Responding to Poems*. London: Routledge.
Carter, R. and Nash, W. (1990) Seeing Through Language, Oxford: Blackwell.
DES (1982) *First School Survey*. London: HMSO.
DES (1988) *The Kingman Report*. London: HMSO.
Glaser, B. and Strauss, A. (1967) *The Discovery of Grounded Theory*. London: Weidenfeld and Nicholson.
Hall, L. (1989) *Poetry for Life*. London: Cassell.
Levin, S. (1962) *Linguistic Structures in Poetry*. The Hague: Moulton.
Touponce, W. (1990) *Literary Theory and the Notion of Difficulty*. New York: Center for the Learning and Teaching of Literature.
Thompson, L. and Millward, P. (1994) Children talking about poetry. In H. Constable, S. Farrow and J. Norton (eds) *Change in Classroom Practice*. Lewes: Falmer Press.

Chapter 2

Poetry as Play: Rules for the Imagination

Gundel Mattenklott
(Translated by Brian Poole)

Long before pictures and images begin to dominate, a child experiences both the calming and stimulating sound of the mother's voice and heartbeat; a child still in the womb is capable of registering these sounds. We know from experience how important the mother's speech and singing is for the early development of the child. This is the case even before the child is capable of understanding the mother's words. From these experiences the child is bathed in a rhythmical, euphonic and melodic stream of speech that is just as important for healthy growth as nourishment and warmth. Although this maternal stream of speech is not poetry, it comes as close to being poetry as the spontaneous and natural can approach a deliberate and planned work of art. It shares some of the qualities of poetry. Freed by the absence of a censorship imposed by the dictates of semantic rationalism, it has rhythm, sound, melody and repetition.

Of course the child does not remain a passive recipient of the mother's flow of speech for long. Julia Kristeva has interpreted the vocal articulations of the infant during the first year. She has noted repetition which is not yet an imitation of the mother's speaking but is triggered by a physical feeling of either discomfort or stress. Between the fourth and the twelfth months the stress is overcome when the child learns to structure the flow of sound (*le flux sonore*) with rhythmic repetitions. Kristeva juxtaposed this early pre-symbolic, rhythmical activity of the child with the literary methods of modernism, which in a different context can lead to a proliferation of textual meanings or, equally possible, to their dissolution. Her comparison reveals forms of highly artificial regression bordering on madness.

But let us return to the children. The widely-spread traditions which schematically represent mother–child interaction in the first months after birth have focused on the narrowest aspects of the poetic elements of the mother's speech, namely nursery rhymes and lullabies. Although it is not possible to comment on individual speech praxis, there are rich collections of early poetry, such as *Des Knaben Wunderhorn*, Mother Goose and many others. Hans Magnus Enzensberger, the editor of an anthology of children's verse, *Allerleirauh*, published in the 1960s, refers to children's verse as *prima poesis*, the first poetry in an individual's life. It accompanies the child from birth, with verses for nappy-changing, bathing and finger games, to the later counting rhymes, word rhymes and jingles which are all part of the independent games of older children. Common to all these forms of poetry is their direct relationship to the body, to movement and gesticulation. The ears, nose, mouth, fingers and feet are touched at rhythmic intervals. In dandling-verse, for example, the whole body is set in motion, the child experiencing the dizzying effects of being bounced about with the chills and thrills of simulated free fall. Finger-play converts the hand into the child's first stage, the fingers into actors. Counting-rhymes make use of the index finger and often include touching the fellow playmates as they are counted off. Other common characteristics of this poetry lie in the predominance of rhythm, alliteration, rhyme and euphony over meaning. In most cases the verses are sheer nonsense.

Small children love this physical play with language, just as they love song. When they begin to attend school we, as teachers, can address and enliven the pleasure the children already find in the rhythm, repetition and sounds of language. Teachers can nurture this pleasure with new poems and verses.

However, in Germany there is a perplexing phenomenon: young people, adolescents and students at universities, even those who study literature, tend to reject poetry. They find that they cannot relate to poetic form and language, and even at times find them tiresome. Given the original pleasure experienced through poetry, how did this rejection develop? If asked, young people point to school as the guilty party. In particular they identify the overwhelmingly analytical and interpretative nature of literature teaching. But since many students who express distaste for poetry nevertheless want to become teachers themselves, I suspect that the defensive reaction against lyric poetry is inherited. It is passed down from generation to generation, from teacher to pupil. It seems to me, therefore, of utmost importance that the buried pleasure of lyric poetry should be rediscovered by future teachers. This is important because as teachers they will need to encourage and foster the innate, quasi-biological pleasure that children experience in poetry.

One step in this direction requires that our eyes be opened to the vast richness of verse which is accessible to children without being boring for adults. The poetry which teachers offer their pupils should have something to say to the teachers as well as the pupils. Children's lyric poetry in the German-speaking community has grown dramatically in the last forty years. It has left behind the narrow confines of childish solicitousness and pedagogic discipline. There are a number of distinguished writers of poetry that has strong appeal for children: Christine Busta, with her slender but demanding volume for children, *Die Sternenmühle* (*The Star Mill*, 1959); James Krüss, the tireless rhymer and pundit with his widely-received works; Josef Guggenmos, who has now turned 70, with his subtle nature-lyrics for children; and, finally, Peter Hacks, a successor of Bertolt Brecht's sovereign command of lyric form combined with humour and invention. Particularly noteworthy is his work, *Der Flohmarkt* (*The Flea Market*, 1965). Together these writers have contributed to the enrichment of children's lyric poetry. Mention should also be made of those authors whose own works for children have been influenced by the movement known internationally since the 1950s as 'concrete poetry'. These include the Swiss writer Hans Manz and the German Burckhard Garbe, to name just two. Among publishers, Hans-Joachim Gelberg, editor for the publishing house Beltz and Gelberg, has perhaps done most for the development of children's lyric poetry in the last twenty years. His anthologies, *Die Stadt der Kinder* (*City of Children*, 1969) and *Überall und neben dir* (*Everywhere and Beside You*, 1986), are both trendsetting. Student teachers can scarcely overestimate the value of these anthologies. They contain a broad range of texts suitable for all kinds of moods and situations. These are texts which actively encourage children in dramatic, musical and artistic engagement.

However, children should not only be read poems that have been specially written for them. Children should also be encouraged to respond receptively to great literary works, traditional and modern. For those who take their pupils seriously, nothing but the best works are good enough. The German public school teacher Ute Andresen, for example, has consistently offered her students the poems that she herself enjoys. She has found difficult poems from the romantic period or earlier to be highly successful with her pupils. She has published transcripts of televised conversations with children which provide evidence that they can profit from the reading of such texts even though they understand them differently from adults. For example, a study of the transcripts reveals that children interpret poems which for adult readers are erotic, on the basis of their own experience with friendships, irrespective of whether these are erotic or not. The prerequisite for such a candid relationship with poetry of all kinds seems to lie in the absence of overt teaching. By dispensing with the concept of there being one, and only one, correct understanding of the text and the rush to get this message across to the children, the teaching has become more successful.

Of course, regular and uncensored reading, as well as the presence of poetry in schools, is all-important; but, beyond the reception of literature, one should not underestimate the children's desire to work actively with language, especially forms of poetry. In Germany in the last twenty years the method of teaching free text has become more and more popular. In particular, using the framework of a new Freinet-reception inspired by French, English and American models has influenced a broad extra-curricular and extra-pedagogical writing movement. This way of teaching literature has the advantage of combining various mutually-complementing concepts.

Literary improvisation

Here I would like to present the concept I began to develop in 1976, provisionally entitled 'Literary Improvisation' (Mattenklott, 1979). It is different from the practice of totally free writing without thematic and formal restrictions and seeks instead to inspire productivity through formal rules and limitations. It is based on a principle which has been practised by countless artists, namely, that fantasy does not develop by drifting in free flight but is forced to develop while wrestling with resistance against the forms and traditions of poetry. The free play of imagination is allowed to test its strength in a game with a limited field of play, a limited time for play, and a set of rules fixed for the game.

I have tested this concept in numerous groups, in schools with children and young adults, and in the field of extra-curricular education with adults of all professions and ages including the elderly, and particularly with students training to be primary school teachers. As an open collection of game-suggestions and rules, literary improvisation can be used successfully at all school levels (and at all ages) with very few adjustments. Here I shall restrict myself to the use of this approach with primary school children aged between six and ten years, and to work with student teachers who are preparing to use this method for work in primary school classrooms.

Literary improvisation for children of primary school age places stress on language play and lyric realization. This appeals to the interest and enjoyment that children of this age group take in language as an inexhaustible and continually accessible material for play: in conundrums and word games, from the serious to the light-hearted, in literalness or ambiguity, in secret languages and pidgin-dialects which they use to simulate foreign languages. I see in these interests a development parallel to the early childhood pleasure with sound, rhyme and words, mentioned at the beginning of this chapter. At the primary school level the pleasure of childhood verse with its characteristic rhythm, repetition and sound-play remains, but is enhanced by the fun of rule-breaking at every level of language including the phonetic, grammatical and syntactic. Children delight in breaking the rules that have only recently been learned.

Language play has other dimensions which demonstrate the significance of these games in teaching. It is an ideal way to develop a conscious awareness of the use of language. In language play, language itself is reflected upon. This practice coincides with the natural interests of children, who like to reflect upon the nature of language, and helps them to develop their own theories about the connection between the signifier and the signified, the word and the object. These are precisely the questions which form the background for many language games. Language play is an important element of all poetry. This can be seen in rhyme and strophic form, allegory and metaphor.

In considering poetry as play, we emphasize not only an activity familiar to the child, but also the performative aspect of poetry. The word play describes two things: it is, on the one hand, something predefined and complete, a complex set of rules, usually including game materials such as cards, a board game, figures, dice, and so on; on the other hand, play is also something with an infinite number of possibilities, a self-renewing process following pre-defined rules, during the course of which the rules themselves can be modified, elaborated or eliminated. The two-sidedness of the game, the one side reflecting back upon the past whilst the other side is directed towards the future, is a quality poetry shares with music. It leaves the interpretative representation of complete and finite compositions room for activity, beginning with repetition and continuing to borderline destruction and recreation. Chomsky has called this movement within the rules, structural change. He regards structural change and rule-changing as evidence of creativity. This is also the case with poetry. Poetry is, as a work of art, something historically finished, but at the same time poetry is actualized in a new and different way with each new reading. Poetry originates by following or breaking rules, and by creating new rules and new impulses for further works.

Games with sound

I shall now give a few examples of lyric language games suitable for use with primary school children. The first suggestion is for a group activity in which the group plays with word sound and language sound. In this activity poetry approaches music. The children learn to focus their attention on the nuances of vowels and the qualities of consonants, both of which are major elements in general language instruction. Analogies in children's games can be found in tongue-twisters, where all the words begin with the same consonant and the consonant is repeated within the sentence as often as possible. 'Peter Piper picked a peck of pickled pepper' is one well-known example. The pupils are asked to write down these tongue-twisters with their consonant repetitions. They do not have to be based on the same sounds, p and k, as in the example cited. Texts obtain an entirely different tonal quality when nasal and liquid consonants dominate. Listen to this German lullaby from the romantic period which gives priority to soft consonant sounds, suggestive of music:

> Singet leise, leise, leise,
> Singt ein flüsternd Wiegenlied,
> Von dem Monde lernt die Weise,
> Der so still am Himmel zieht.
>
> Singt ein Lied so süß gelinde,
> wie die Quellen auf den Kieseln,
> wie die Bienen um die Linde ...

Another example of a song that children love to sing is 'Dra Chanasan mat dam Kantrabaß'. It repeats a single stanza five times with five different vowels, followed by five different diphthongs. The rules for the game require pupils to write a text in which there is only one *a*, one *e*, one *i*, one *o*, or one *u*. The Austrian lyric writer Ernst Jandl, one of the most prominent contemporary authors writing in German, has composed a poem 'Ottos Mops' using only one vowel, '*o*'. As they get to know these works, children begin to regard such authors as colleagues as they produce their own vowel texts; the children's own poems are not always of inferior quality.

Another game requires that one specified vowel is not allowed. Proof that masterpieces have been created in this way can be found in Georges Perec's novel, *La Disparition*, a novel without the vowel *e*. This serious form of literary play is called a lipogram. After all, play with gibberish can be turned into a literally productive game. The Dadaist Hugo Ball's interlinguistic poems offer an example of work which can be combined with dramatic improvisation; one example is 'Seepferdchen und Flugfische' ('Seahorses and Flying Fish'). It requires no translation.

> tressli bessli nebogen leila
> flusch kata
> ballubasch
> zack hitti zopp
>
> zack hitti zopp
> hitti betzli betzli
> prusch kata ...

Games with letters

Another successful teaching activity is to ask a group to collect games with letters. Here poetry approaches pictorial art. The games encourage the acquisition of written language and are well adapted to children's developing theories and experiments with letters. Letter names and the alphabet are frequently the topic of children's games, and this activity extends this interest. The ABC (Abecedarius) is a poem based upon the order of the alphabet. Even though, nowadays, the alphabet is no longer the central focus of study in the primary school, it still remains essential. Many renowned authors have written poetic ABCs. These include Edward Lear, Wilhelm Busch and Bertolt Brecht, to name just a few. Their rhymed texts either tell stories or have a special theme, such as animals or political catchwords. For both children and adults, the task of finding a simple thematically-related string of words in alphabetical order is difficult enough. But the string of words can, nonetheless, be poetic: one need only rediscover the relish of enumeration as a traditional literary device (I am thinking especially of the use of lists in the works of Rabelais and James Joyce). A love poem by Friederike Mayröcker, perhaps the greatest contemporary woman poet in the German language, is an enumeration of affectionate words; it is just one example of this kind of poem.

> Wie ich dich nenne
> Wenn ich an dich denke
> und du nicht da bist:
>
> meine Walderdbeere
> meine Zuckerechse
> meine Trosttüte
> mein Seidenspinner ...

But to return to the alphabet, and in particular to those games with the alphabet that allow children to experience their enjoyment in pictorial representation and graphic ornamentation. The decorative and inventive representation of letters not only continues an established theme in western culture in handwritten books (the ornamentation of initial letters, for example). It is also an art well adapted to aid the development of children's ability to work in a meaningful and aesthetically satisfying way with two-dimensional representation, while also developing their own individually stylized handwriting.

Another game with letters is the acrostic, which in its simplest form uses names as texts. The child is asked to write the letters of his or her name in a vertical line and then to find words that begin with those letters. This game encourages the children to introduce themselves, adding personalized descriptions such as: what I like to eat, what I wish most of all, what I want to become, and so on. Writing acrostics can also be a classroom activity with older pupils, using the tradition of the acrostic as a form of dedication or love poem, in which the first letter of each line yields the name of the addressee. Such suggestive forms of poetry are well suited to one's first secret love and the delight in encoded messages and hidden initials. Such a poetry-writing activity can give rise to projects to which pupils respond with great enthusiasm. Like all other games with letters, the acrostic game, which both conceals and reveals the name of the beloved, dates back to the mystical traditions written in celebration, but avoiding mention, of the holy, and tabooed, name of God.

Another step towards pictorial representation can be achieved through the creation of figure-texts and picture-poems, the oldest of which were handed down from ancient times. In these poems the words are organized so that the form of the words renders the content visible. By rendering their meaning in these two ways, in words and an image, picture-poems reflect a regression to the early forms of literate culture. The poems seem to skirt the progressive step achieved by abstract written language and return to the original object-related image-writing. The twentieth century is particularly fascinated by play with writing in works of literature, for example in the graphic arts, and even in experimental music using unconventional notation. These are art forms which cross the traditional borderlines separating the arts and, like the works of Artaud and James Joyce (Julia Kristeva compared them to the early vocalization of infants), produce a surplus of meaning while at the same time giving expression to the dismantling of the meaning.

Those involved with teaching writing to children have in recent years fostered the theory that children, while learning to write, retrace various phases and develop ideas akin to the history of written language. By setting them the task of depicting the meaning of words and texts with letters and pictures, the practice of teaching writing coincides with the theory of the history of writing and allows the children to become conversant with a thousand-year-old tradition which is still alive in modern art. Calligraphies such as Apollinaire's famous 'Il pleut' are immediately accessible to children and encourage them both to imitate and to create their own. Of course, mention should also be made of the 'Mouse's Tail' poem from *Alice in Wonderland* which is yet another example. Since Alice is a descendant of Ariadne, she is perhaps the best guide through the labyrinth of language games.

This last metaphor of the labyrinth is my cue for the next game. Set within the framework of figure-texts, letter labyrinths are known to us from the early Diskos of Phaistos. Children are already familiar with labyrinths in a number of ways. They know them through games like leap-frog and puzzles and puzzle-books. In letter games the children create their own labyrinths, through which the reader must twist and turn around in order to decipher the meaning. Children can hide all sorts of humour, horror and surprises in their labyrinths.

Pictorial texts refer back to yet another early phase in the history of writing, the pre-linear age. Our children gain direct experience of this while playing with one of the aesthetic principles of modernism, for example, the liberation of words from any formal meaning. The French poet Mallarmé took a decisive step toward emancipating words on the page, as did Marinetti in his Futurist Manifesto, when he formulated their battle-cry: *Parole en liberté*. Liberated words acquire a poetic life of their own which distinguishes them from those words which are forced into the service of the sentence and logical order, the bureaucrats of language and writing. Let loose in the endless play of associations and combinations, liberated words either rule like absolute princes or can turn to anarchy on the page. Their letters can stretch and enlarge themselves or shrink up.

Typographical experiments with the help of ink pads and the classroom press, collages of newspaper headlines, text fragments and colour, can all be put to good use in these games. And why should we limit children to two-dimensional surfaces? We ought to consider the plans from Raymundus Lullus and Athanasius Kirchner, and more recently from the school of contemporary object and concept artists, for machines which supplement the world of writing by adding the dimension of space in order to simplify the search for metaphors and enrich the art of poetry with rare and surprising language images. We can build mobiles out of words. Their perpetual movement yields word combinations that produce a new poem every time they move. Justification for the kind of literary study that helps children learn to appreciate and understand these types of poetry as art, can be said to belong within the larger framework of aesthetic education.

Games with word meanings

I shall now leave the subject of letter games and take up the subject of games with word meanings. Children as beginners in language are, of course, much more attentive than adults to the conventionalized images in our languages. Adults are inclined not to notice the literal sense of words that children are just beginning to use. But if children are asked to write stories and paint pictures in which they use figurative expressions in a literal sense, we are suddenly confronted with someone who really is all ears, someone else who can really lie through his teeth, someone who is as solid as a rock, and perhaps even with a slightly less congenial lady strangely resembling a battle-axe. Such games provide adults with the opportunity to rediscover the colourfulness of seemingly jaded idioms and children with the opportunity to learn to dig more deeply into the pictorial dimension of language.

Lewis Carroll's *Alice in Wonderland* and *Alice Through the Looking-Glass* are perhaps the best examples of a game that involves literal and figurative meaning. We need only imagine a fairy-tale-like bestiary in which Alice's mock turtle, her bread-and-butter-fly, her rocking-horse-fly and her snap-dragon-fly take their place of honour. In the same neighbourhood as this bestiary are Humpty-Dumpty's portmanteau-words (you see, it is like a portmanteau – there are two meanings packed into one word). These are the words that so amused the surrealists and eventually found their way into *Finnegan's Wake*, that bible of language games. All these literary works provide teachers with examples of words displaying their inexhaustible potency.

Finally, we must consider homonyms in lyric poetry. These have been popular since the nineteenth century. Homonyms are often responsible for the plurality of meanings created within a poem. For example, in his poem 'Auf eine Lampe' ('On a Lamp'), the romantic poet Mörike plays upon the different meanings of the verb *scheinen*, which in German can mean to shine (to emit light) or to seem to be, to appear, to occur to one (in the sense of an epiphany). It is also a word frequently associated with the discussion of aesthetics. Mörike's usage is not unique. It can be found among his contemporary philosophers. A love poem of another German poet of the twentieth century vacillates between images of the tonsils in the throat and the almonds of an almond tree (in German tonsils and almonds are one and the same word). Raymond Roussel has based his theory of poetry and his literary *œuvre* on homonyms. Michel Leiris is another poet who has not only created his own glossary of words with the same or similar sound ('Langage tangage ou ce que les mots me disent', and 'Glossaire j'y serre mes gloses', are just two examples), but has also followed this subtle use of language in the volume entitled *Biffures* which forms part of his psychoanalytical autobiography, *La Régle du Jeu*. Such word-play is very familiar to German children in the form of a puzzle game called the little teapot, the object of which is to guess, on the basis of definitions, the homonym in question. This game can set a collective poetic process in motion in which the entire class gathers meaning through associated words and word-fields for a specific homonym. We then use the collection, with its myriad connections at different levels of meaning, to write new texts. These homonym exercises enrich vocabulary while at the same time offering a short, introductory crash course in metaphor.

Games with rhyme

The last group of language games I would like to present relates to poetic imitation in the narrowest sense of the word. All children seem to be fascinated by rhyme. One German author, Peter Rühmkorf, wrote in the early 1980s a small natural history of rhyme which drew attention overtly to the occurrence of rhyme in everyday speech, and its special function in the fashion industry and particularly in advertising. His examples sharpen our awareness of the pre-literary rhyme that young children use in their speech. Rhyme can perform a number of functions. It can join semantically unequal words in harmonic sound (Herman Meyer has rewritten the history of rhyme as the history of a love and marriage metaphor, for example). Or, by contrast, rhyme can emphasize the incompatible dissonances in similarly-sounding words. This is a particular feature of modern poetry. Rhyme also plays a significant role in the social life of primary school children – one need only consider behaviour such as teasing and name-calling to be aware of this. In their own lyrical culture of scatological and sexual risqué verse, which is so often concealed from the ears of adults, children demonstrate a rich sense of wit and imagination in forging rhymes.

There is also a wealth of small games based upon this kind of verbal behaviour. For example, texts in which the rhyme must be continued, or rhyming in a circle which follows a model verse. Rhyming pairs is perhaps the most simple game. But children are also capable of more complex rhyme systems and models. The limerick is an example which falls into this category; Edward Lear's *Nonsense Verse* was a tremendous success even as a children's book. Susanne Ehmcke's *Reimallein* (*The Rhyme-alone*) is another lyric cycle suitable for children. It was first published in 1964, but since then has been unjustly forgotten. It offers a series of limericks which are ideal small poems for young children to imitate. The hero, the Rhyme-alone, is a small boy, pictorially represented in the book, who appears in a series of verses in which he encounters all sorts of things which lead eventually to all kinds of discussions that seem to arise out of the rhyme itself. The author prefaces her graceful verse stories with a poetic agenda that also appears in limerick form:

> Auf Baum reimt sich Traum, und auf Besen,
> da reimt sich gar mancherlei Wesen.
> Seltsame Geschichten
> entstehen beim Dichten –
> Man wundert sich manchmal beim Lesen.

In conclusion it should be remembered that rhyme is a powerful source of thought, a poetic inspiration-machine. In rhyme and play we follow in the footsteps of the muses, although we somehow never seem to learn their secret, which resides in the autonomous activity of language as it passes through the individual poet.

As children get older they progress from playing school games. However, it is these games that have taught them the foundations of rhyme, metre and stanza. Their early word-games offer an introduction to the great lyric traditions. The first of these games uses the sonnet, which, as a form of literary communication, can draw upon an extensive tradition. In the French salons of the seventeenth century, the *bouts-rimés* (initial rhymes which were to be completed in sonnet form) were quite popular. Tercets, octaves (*octava rima*), and rondels are among the lyric forms which were traditionally part of a larger social activity in which the roles of reader and writer overlapped.

In the reciprocal play between reading and one's own lyric production, schools can become workshops for developing literature. Language education, teaching literature and the literary avant-garde would not be so estranged from one another if teachers and pupils would follow the goal laid out by OuLiPo – *Ouvroir de littérature potentielle* (Workshop for Potential Literature) – an international group of authors founded by Raymond Queneau, to which Italo Calvino, Jacques Roubaud and Georges Perec belong. The organization is interested in broadening the literary system of rules and in systematic research of sources of poetic inspiration. When children become acquainted with poems and learn to develop their own early on, we, as teachers, can educate them to be mature readers who no longer read simply content, but are familiar with the secrets of the literary forms in which content obtains the aesthetic quality that is beyond science and day-to-day speech and that renders a work of art irreplaceable.

REFERENCES

Andresen, Ute (1992) *Versteh mich nicht so schnell: Gedichte lesen mit Kindern*. Weinheim: Berlin.
Ball, Hugo (1963) *Gesammelte Gedichte*. Zürich: Anche.
Kristeva, Julia (1977) Contraintes rythmiques et langage poétique. In *Polylogue*, Paris: Seuil.
Mattenklott, Gundel (1979) *Literarische Geselligkeit* (Schreiben in der Schule). Stuttgart: Metzler.
Mayröcker, Friederike (1989) *Zittergaul*. Ravensberg: Otto Maier.
Meyer, Herman (1987) Erotik des Reimes. In *Spiegelungen: Studien zu Literatur und Kunst*. Tübingen: Niemeyer.
Rühmkorf, Peter (1981) *Agar agar: zaurzaurim. Zur Naturgeschichte des Reims und der menschlichen Anklangsnerven*. Reinbek bei Hamburg: Ruwohlt.

Chapter 3

Reading Poetry and Primary School Practice

Linda Hall

I do not think that I am misrepresenting current school practice if I say that poetry does not enjoy a prominent place in the curriculum of our primary and secondary schools. Indeed, various authorities testify to its widespread neglect.[1] However, when it does make an all-too-fleeting appearance, it is unfortunately subjected to methods and approaches which distort and damage its very special qualities and seem to make it without exception the most detested subject that children meet during their schooldays.

Mention the word 'poetry' to a group of adults and the response you evoke is at best cool indifference, at worst plain hostility. There is no doubt that poetry is perceived by most people, including many teachers, as something highbrow, difficult and obscure. Government reports and surveys support this impression and make depressing reading. It is no exaggeration to say that poetry seems to generate more antipathy in secondary pupils, particularly among boys, than does the supposedly dreaded maths. More than fifteen years ago the Bullock Report (DES, 1975) cited a survey which found that of 1,000 O- and A-level candidates only 17 per cent thought they might venture to read any more poetry after leaving school. More recently the Assessment of Performance Unit's first report, *Language Performance in Schools: a Secondary Survey*, noted that more than three quarters of all school leavers were indifferent to poetry and as many as 36 per cent confessed to hating it. Poetry's status as 'a minor amenity but a major channel of experience' (DES, 1963: 156), recorded thirty years ago in *Half Our Future* (DES, 1963), a report of the then Ministry of Education, is a lamentable fact of life, even in the one place where it could enjoy considerable favour – that is, in school.

At the primary level, where the element of enjoyment in reading poetry is not dissipated by the business of studying poems for examination purposes, one might think that poetry would be more likely to be popular. Such is not the case. Indeed, I intend to argue in this chapter that the problem in the primary school (where poetry could really come into its own) is that current primary practices are in fact inimical to its success as a subject. The difficulty lies in the fact that certain ideas and approaches which predominate at present at the primary level ignore the intrinsic value of poetry and fail to pay it the respect that it deserves and needs if it is to work its magic on children. I have in mind notions like relevance, which limits choice of material; the topic-based approach which dictates a particularly restricted way of looking at a poem; the idea that 'activity' is the normal and natural need of the primary school child's working day, which ignores and even downgrades the quietly internal nature of poetry's appeal to the imagination and feelings; the 'stimulus and response' method of promoting children's 'creative' writing, which largely excludes the introduction of rhymed poetry to children because 'free verse' is an easier form to imitate. Each one of these ideas needs to be critically addressed, but in one chapter of this length, that is not going to be possible. However, I shall attempt to indicate briefly the deleterious effects they have had on poetry teaching and try to suggest why reading poetry *for its own sake* is so vitally important, particularly at the primary level.

In fact, I want to make the case for reading poetry in a way that is not common practice as yet in our primary schools. Even when poetry does appear fitfully in our classrooms, it is not generally read *for itself alone*, or as a subject *in its own right*. It is rarely allowed to speak for itself and this is especially true at the primary level. Current and entrenched primary practices like those mentioned earlier actually detract from a poem ever getting through in its own voice to the pupils exposed to it. This is because these teaching methods are both intrusive and instrumentalist.

The Bullock Report (DES, 1975: 388) noted that 44 per cent of nine-year-olds spent up to (and no more than) thirty minutes per week on poetry. This statistic might not be thought to offer evidence of neglect, but what Bullock failed to indicate was the *context* in which this poetry reading occurred. It is important to know if it was introduced to pupils simply on the basis of its own intrinsic pleasures (for example, the experience of words well used) or if its presence was dictated by the need to use it as *a means to an end*. My guess is that it was present briefly in the classrooms that Bullock observed in order to provide a stimulus for the children's own writing of poetry, or as an illustration in verse form of a theme in project or topic work. For this has been the status accorded poetry when it appears in our primary schools – to be a mere means to an end rather than an end in itself.

It is surprising that the modern concern with creativity has led to the kind of teaching of poetry that would warm the heart of Mr Gradgrind himself. For poetry is incorporated into lessons only to serve a strictly utilitarian purpose. It is rarely read for its own sake, as something of value in its own right. The intrinsic worth of a poem that is 'used' (and I write the word deliberately) as stimulus or illustration is inevitably missed. In the attempt to goad children into their own creativity, the poet's own creative efforts and our pupils' pleasure in his achievement go for naught. To 'use' poetry for such purposes fails to allow pupils the opportunity to 'stand and stare' in admiration and wonder at a poem, to savour its language, to ponder its thoughts and immerse themselves in its emotion. Poetry's own special qualities, which would win children over to reading it, are not given a chance to germinate in their hearts and minds.

The Pavlovian 'stimulus and response' model of teaching poetry that lies behind the usual 'read-talk-write-your-own' format has become inflexible. It also fails to take into account the special nature of poetry, which can provoke quite unexpected reactions. For example, one of the many possible responses after hearing a poem read aloud is silence. Our teaching strategies do not normally allow for this, especially not at the primary level. That children do not attempt to articulate a response may well be a tribute to the depths to which the poem has touched them. It need not be lack of interest nor a failure of understanding, even though that understanding may be only hesitant and intuitive. So often we, as teachers, break the delicate butterfly of a child's apprehension of a poem on the rack of our commitment to lay bare the meanings that we perceive in it. This is particularly true of the topic or project approach.

Walter de la Mare reminds us, in his interesting introduction to his anthology *Come Hither*, that one of the pleasures of reading is that

> you may make any picture out of the words that you can or will; and a poem may have as many different meanings as there are different minds to read it.
> (de la Mare, 1953: xxxiii)

Poems are such many-faceted artefacts and a child's first engagement with them is such a private affair, even when mediated by a teacher's reading, that the teaching strategies we adopt should be sufficiently sensitive and restrained to allow our pupils to retain their own perceptions intact. This must mean a recognition that it is not a necessary outcome of reading poetry that children should venture to write their own. This is particularly so in the primary years, when interest in reading is still at the burgeoning stage. HMI suggests this is so even at the secondary level:

> The outcome of poetry teaching need not be writing at all and many poems can be read just for themselves, as an experience of the moment whose echoes for some will last into the future.
> (DES, 1987: 29)

To use poetry to illustrate a set theme virtually denies the range of responses proposed by de la Mare above and again pins a poem down to the teacher's own partial interpretation of its implications. Such a practice fails to allow pupils room to think and feel their way into a poem for themselves, but circumscribes their responses from the outset.

There is an even greater loss when poetry is subjected to inclusion in project or thematic work. What is lost sight of is that experience of literature for its own sake which alone seems to develop children into enthusiastic readers. What I mean by this is the experience of comparing the present poem with another that pupils have previously enjoyed, of reflecting on their own similar experiences of life and literature, in short, of 'anticipating and retrospecting' (Benton and Fox, 1987: 106). I am not alone when I assert that it is only possible for children to develop a life-long love of reading literature if it is presented as something of value and interest in its own right. But when covert utilitarian purposes dictate its presence in a lesson and fix its possible meanings, pupils quickly deduce that poetry is just another teaching tool like a textbook and moderate their interest accordingly.

The following anecdote is interesting in this context. Some years ago the topic or (at the secondary level) thematic approach tended to be sociologically biased. I recall the occasion when I witnessed a student teacher introduce 'The Wraggle Taggle Gypsies' in order to discuss the pros and cons of government legislation concerning gypsy sites. Now sociology is in decline and science holds sway, but poetry is still seen through the equally distorting prism of another subject area. My students in teacher education courses nowadays come to me requesting that I recommend poems about Light and Air or Forces.

The practice of using poetry for other ends, which is still so popular at the primary level, embodies a hitherto unrecognized 'hidden curriculum' which is very disturbing. It means that a poem does not have to be worth reading for its own sake; it does not even have to be a good poem. Its value lies in how far it links up with the current topic or theme. This exploitative approach inevitably bypasses the best poems and reduces imaginative literature, with all its potentially emotional and intellectual benefits, to an arid functionalism. It thereby presents young children with an insidiously dangerous model. This exploitation of poetry simply mirrors and reinforces the values of the commercially exploitative world that exists outside the school gates and can only help to prepare our pupils to accept exploitation as the norm in life. Access to poetry, on the other hand, offers us values that are diametrically opposed to that exploitative world, in the way that it puts us in tune with the heart and the spirit. Our practice must attempt to reflect poetry's humane values.

It is clear that in the last two decades 'the unique value of literature which can be discovered only through its unique disciplines' (Bolt and Gard, 1970: 148) has been sacrificed on the altar of a reductionist utilitarianism. Unfortunately, such approaches have also become entrenched.

However, if we regard poetry as an end in itself, what follows is liberation from such restrictions as described above. A poetry lesson can then legitimately be quite self-contained and does not have to lead anywhere or stimulate anything except an interest in poetry and pleasure in *reading* it. Reading is the operative word. Not necessarily writing one's own, or answering comprehension questions or discussing its meaning. Teacher reads aloud, pupil volunteers read aloud, sharing our appreciation by means of expressive reading.

All a teacher needs to do in fact is to read lots of poems aloud expressively and with feeling, so that what poets have to say can reach the children unimpeded. The poem itself will do the rest, weave its magic quite unaided, and certainly does not need a teacher's constant intervention by means of comprehension questions, discussion points and writing tasks. No amount of expressive activities will reveal how effectively or deeply a poem has touched the inner recesses of a child's being. There are creative responses that go on within a pupil's heart and mind that we cannot see in operation nor quantify in outward signs or by expressive activities.

For these creative responses to occur, a poem needs freedom and its own space in order to exercise its particular appeal. It cannot be tied to another subject. A good expressive reading is the only bit of ritual that is needed to put pupils in touch with the feelings, thoughts, language, form, rhyme and rhythm that go to make a poem. Restraint is in fact the cardinal rule here. However, current primary practices militate against the simplicity and delicacy of what I am recommending. Let me add that what I am suggesting does not mean that we reject children's own questions or comments on the poems we read aloud to them. Reading poems may well provoke spontaneous reminiscence from pupils and that is not to be discouraged.

I once witnessed John Clare's 'The Pettichap's Nest' evoke feeling comments from 11-year-old boys about finding eggs and young fledglings that had fallen out of their nests. Such personal remarks are legitimate because they reveal pupils responding sensitively to the emotional content of the poem and sharing those feelings. They were still with the poem, so to speak, still thinking and feeling within its imaginative ambit. This is an important consideration because there is a tendency in primary education today, obsessed as it is with 'doing', to be forever leading the lesson far away from its starting point. The habit is to use a poem merely as a springboard to promote talk, however inconsequential, and to link up with art, drama, dance or craftwork. Yet as Clive Sansom (1978: 120) rightly points out, 'drawing or acting may externalize something which is best left to the imagination'.

It is all a matter of tact. It is quite feasible and proper that occasionally one's poetry lesson should involve drama or art, but not as a regular occurrence. It is important to recognize which poems genuinely submit themselves to drama (those with refrains, choruses and dialogue), or have a strong visual quality or merely lend themselves to a shared and feeling response. Some, of course, are best left to silence.

Poetry reading is essentially about listening and its requisite stillness, not about activity. It involves quieter internal pleasures of a deeply personal, even private, kind. If response comes unbidden from some children, all well and good. But teacher attempts at explanation or discussion can often spoil a child's own personal response or private dream. We can never tell just what pictures and feelings a poem may have evoked for a child. To require our pupils to articulate the golden glow deep down inside or the sense of recognition that a poem has given is ultimately destructive, as L. A. G. Strong pointed out more than forty years ago:

> Explanations and annotations do not matter. A child's misconceptions may be of much greater value to him than the explanation which destroys it. I have heard more than once a heartfelt cry, 'Oh, Sir, please don't explain it!' which showed that imagination had been bruised already by the smashing of a cherished mental picture. Only a pedant will, in such instances, value accuracy above the magic which some word or phrase is exercising on a young imagination.
> (1946: 11–12)

To paraphrase Wordsworth, there are thoughts that do often lie too deep for words, especially when coming across them for the first time. This applies to all people of all ages and not just to children. Poetry is one of the few subject areas of the curriculum that deals with intangibles. When it is read expressively by a teacher and is successfully getting through to its listeners, it works in ways that cannot really be assessed or quantified. What I am suggesting is so straightforward and simple. Children listen to a poet's words, the expression of his or her heart and soul, through the medium of the teacher's voice. Such an approach, despite its simplicity, can never be boring or predictable because poets vary so much one from another. What few teachers seem to realize is that poetry can be safely left to win its audience by its own power and does not need our interventionist or instrumentalist policies.

As I think my foregoing comments have already implied, poetry is of indisputable value at the primary level because of its potential for nourishing our pupils' emotional and imaginative lives. What I have not so far mentioned is that when it is used with deliberation, poetry also has a vital capacity for enlarging young children's awareness of the rich resources of the English language. A recent HMI document has stressed the central role that poetry plays in promoting the language development of our pupils and in doing so echoes Matthew Arnold's definition of poetry as a *quality of language*:

> Poetry needs to be at the heart of work in English because of the quality of language at work on experience that it offers to us ... It is the place of poetry in English teaching to help us to restore to pupils a sense of the exuberance and vitality in the acquisition of language and in the power and savour of words.
> (DES, 1987: 3)

Although these words come from a report about poetry at the secondary level, what they have to say about language development is of even greater significance for the primary years, the period when, as work in brain studies reveals, 'the ability to learn is at flood readiness' (Brierley, 1987: 29). However, in my view this benefit can only accrue to our pupils when poetry is read for its own sake, so that its special linguistic and formal qualities can be paid due attention.

Moreover, when a teacher is not shackled by functionalism in her choice of material, she can select poetry that offers a stimulating experience of language rather than the lacklustre, prosy verse that finds its way into topic-based work. Poets like Shakespeare, whose use of language exhibits a wondrous verve and daring, can be recruited to her lessons. Chukovsky (1971), the great Russian educator, children's writer and pioneer researcher into pre-school children's language, pointed out as long ago as 1919 that the influence of rhymed poetry on young children is to enrich their grasp of the vocabulary and structures of their native tongue.

As we all know, language development and intellectual development are inextricably linked. The more children are exposed to a rich linguistic resource like poetry the better it will be for their own individual language acquisition and burgeoning intellectual capacity. Ideally this should begin with nursery rhymes in the pre-school period, but it is certainly not too late to start in the infants or even juniors. For this reason alone it is of vital importance that primary pupils read poetry for its own sake on a regular basis.

I come now to the final and perhaps most interesting point I wish to make. Recent research into early reading difficulties in primary age children also seems to offer evidence to support the need for a more thoroughgoing inclusion of poetry reading in the primary school curriculum. This research consists of a major longitudinal study of more than 400 children (Bryant and Bradley, 1985). It shows that children who have experienced nursery rhymes and rhymed poetry generally (like that of A. A. Milne) in the pre-school phase have no trouble learning to read when they start school, and develop fluency sooner than others. This is because the presence of phonological patterns like alliteration and rhyme promotes in children the capacity for recognizing sounds that are similar or the same.

Conversely the research found that weakness in phonological awareness at the age of four to five is a significant predictor of a child's later difficulties in learning to read, write or spell. If this is so in the earliest stages of schooling, it must also raise urgent questions as to the place of poetry reading in developing reading skills and fluency throughout the primary years. It certainly seems to argue for a much more central and more frequent presence for poetry in the primary and middle school curricula.

At the first international conference of the British Dyslexia Association (BDA)[2] it was reported that Bryant and Bradley's research has made it 'possible to identify very early on children who are going to run into problems with reading and writing'. Dyslexia is usually regarded as difficult to diagnose until a child is at least seven years old, but what is also important about this research is that it shows that appropriate teaching can bring about a marked improvement. By following the development of a group of children from before they embarked on learning to read, the team could predict from their low scores on rhyming ability which children were likely to encounter reading, writing and spelling problems. A selected group of such children were given a little extra help in making connections between letter patterns and sound patterns. This help amounted in total to only seven hours over a period of two years, yet the children helped in this way made significant progress compared with the control group. It was clear, though, that 'phonic help on its own was not enough' (*TES*, 7 April 1989). In other words, continued reading of a wide range of rhyming poetry and verse is also vital and, in the case of children with learning difficulties, must go hand in hand with appropriate teaching strategies.

The implications of this research appear to be borne out by test scores recorded in *Primary Education in England* (DES, 1978), which found that 'stories and poems were read to children in a higher proportion of the classes with above-average NFER reading scores than in other classes'. (Quoted in *TES*, 7 April 1989.)

This survey could not, of course, tell us if it was a regular diet of poetry that produced better reading scores or if it was simply that abler readers were allowed contact with poetry, usually deemed more demanding than prose. Taken with the research findings, however, these reading scores offer an interesting gloss on the issue.

This research also raises questions about the kind of poetry we read to our pupils. The need to choose rhymed poetry is obviously vital. But it is true to say that when poetry appears in lessons it is more likely to be in the form of free verse, which does not rhyme or even have a rhythm. This would not be such a problem if poetry reading were a more regular occurrence at primary level. But at the present time its appearance is so intermittent that it cannot possibly help to promote the reading skills indicated in the research. It is because free verse has no metrical regularity that it is deemed to be easy to imitate when children have to write their own poetry. Since it has no metrical regularity it lacks the memorableness of rhymed and metrically regular poetry and verse. It is this memorableness of the metrical form which itself imposes on the poet greater deliberation and compression of language than in prose, makes the metaphors and similes sing and so enriches our pupils' awareness of the potentialities of English as their native language. The poet's fascination with the sheer magic of words and his or her pleasure in the shape and pattern conferred by metre and rhyme is shared by all young primary age children. I remember that my own son, aged barely two years, loved to recite words like 'fancy' and 'certainly' (which he had heard in A. A. Milne's 'The King's Breakfast') as if they had talismanic power.

In the very first instance poetry must involve pleasure and delight, especially for primary age pupils. Without that initial attraction they will never have access to its many other benefits. But 'free verse', which Vernon Scannell (1987) has aptly said mostly resembles 'inferior prose', is quite inappropriate, because it cannot satisfy children's rhythmic appetites. Poetry's earliest and main appeal is to the *ear* through rhythm, rhyme and metre. We should not underestimate the intense satisfaction young children derive from the music and ritual of sound as expressed in traditional poetic forms. It is through such aural pleasure that we catch the interest of our pupils. For this reason, so-called free verse has no place in poetry lessons at the primary level.

In conclusion, it is my contention that poetry is of vital importance for our primary pupils, but that present practice, informed by instrumentalist and utilitarian ideas, is actively preventing poetry becoming the most popular subject in the primary (English) school curriculum. While the usual functionalist purposes are afoot, the appreciation of words well used and the delight in rhythm and rhyme which constitute two of the principal pleasures of reading poetry cannot be granted much opportunity to germinate.

NOTES

1. See K. Calthrop and J. Ede, *Not Daffodils Again: Teaching Poetry 9–13* (Longman, 1984); *Teaching Poetry in the Secondary School: An HMI View* (DES, 1987); *The First School Survey* (DES, 1982); *9–13 Middle Schools* (DES, 1983); *Education 8–12 in Combined and Middle Schools* (DES, 1985); *Primary Education in England* (DES, 1978); and last but not least the Bullock Report, *A Language for Life* (DES, 1975).
2. As reported in *The Times Educational Supplement*, 7 April 1989.

REFERENCES

Benton, M. and Fox, G. (1987) *Teaching Literature 9–14*. Oxford: Oxford University Press.
Bolt, S. and Gard, R. (1970) *Teaching Fiction in Schools*. London: Hutchinson.
Brierley, J. (1987) *Give Me a Child Till He Is Seven*. Lewes: Falmer Press.
Bryant, P. and Bradley, L. (1985) *Children's Reading Problems*. Oxford: Blackwell.
de la Mare, W. (1953) *Come Hither*. London: Constable.
Chukovsky, K. (1971) *From Two to Five*. Berkeley: University of California Press.

DES (1963) *Half Our Future – A Report of the Central Advisory Council for Education.* London: HMSO.
DES (1975) *A Language for Life* (Bullock Report). London: HMSO.
DES (1987) *Teaching Poetry in the Secondary School: An HMI View.* London: HMSO.
Sansom, C. (1978) *Speech and Communication in the Primary School.* London: Black.
Scannell, Vernon (1987) *How to Enjoy Poetry.* London: Piaktus.
Strong, L. A. G. (1946) Poetry in the school. In V. da Sola Pinto (ed.) *The Teaching of English in Schools.* London: Macmillan.

Chapter 4

Ways of Experiencing Poetry and Acquiring Poetic Knowledge in Secondary School

Thorkild Borup Jensen

It is a common prejudice among Danish secondary school teachers that poetry is difficult, and they are therefore reluctant to teach it. This is a pity for the teachers and the pupils, as well as for the poems, for poetry represents essential human qualities.

Poems call for our attention and for our co-operation. They want us to go exploring with sharpened senses and alert imagination.

> I dwell in Possibility –
> A fairer House than Prose –
> More numerous of Windows –
> Superior – for Doors –
> Emily Dickinson, *Poem 657*

Poems, in other words, want us to meet life somewhere, as something quite new. What is going on is fundamental, like everyday life, but it is strange and unheard of, all the same.

> I wander chilly and bloodforsaken
> and snap at the sunset.
> Widescreen! Hollywood! Technicolor!
> And glare down at the flagstones
> stamped with greasy leaves
>
> Then a chestnut cracks at my feet.
> A bright brown eye opens.
> Behold heaven and earth
> for the first time.
> Benny Andersen, *Widescreen*

It is easy for us to say that poetry possesses and incorporates a rich world of experiences. But how do we communicate this in the classroom without spoiling the intermediate vitality of the poems and the youngsters' bright curiosity?

WAYS OF EXPERIENCING POETRY

I will suggest some ways of *experiencing poetry* in the classroom which, in my opinion, appeal to the pupils' curiosity and also open up passages into the land of poetry. Most of the suggestions may already be familiar to teachers. Most of them may even be rather ordinary. In fact they have nothing to do with far-fetched, artful strategies. This is deliberate. Teachers should feel that they can do these activities in their own classrooms.

First of all, I should like to suggest singing together in the classroom. This activity could include a variety of songs: well-known and popular songs, as well as quite new unknown ones, the children's own songs and adult songs. Songs to the morning, the day or whatever. Further, having a songbook for everyone in the class is an idea I strongly recommend. There are a number of ways in which songs can be used in the classroom. For example, the teacher could begin with a short introduction to the song that has been chosen. After the class has sung it together the teacher may conclude with a few words on why she is fond of that particular song and why it was chosen. As time goes by and the class becomes more accustomed to this activity, the teacher can pass the responsibility for the choice of the daily song to the pupils, who in turn will be expected to provide a brief introduction to the song of their choice. This activity is an important introduction to poetry because the pupils need to make the connections between poetry and music. It is important to reinforce the impression that poems are accompanied by music and melodic sounds. It is worth reminding ourselves of the meaning of the Greek word *lyric*: 'meant for or sung to the lyre's accompaniment'.

As a related activity I should like to recommend listening to songs on record or audio-tape. These could include both the teacher's and the pupils' favourite songs and performers. After listening together in our class we exchange comments on the tune and the style of singing. We discuss the match between the lyric and the music and explore together what we feel the song gave us.

A third way of experiencing poetry has to do with the poetic knowledge that the children bring with them into the classroom. (See Chapter 1.) As a class we collect and jointly present the jingles and nursery rhymes that we already know and are familiar with. Sometimes we write down some of the rhymes. This work can be done in small groups. Afterwards we discuss what these rhymes have in common, what they are used for now, and how and why we enjoyed them. Demonstrating this enjoyment of poetry in the classroom is important because it brings poetry to life for the pupils. Moving the body to the rhythms and rhymes is an important way of animating the poetry. It is recommended as a way of getting hold of the magic and mystery connected with poems. It is a good way, too, of perceiving the poetic idiom. Poems really do want to do something to us. They want to appeal to our motor senses. They want to make us move. One way of understanding poetry is to look upon poems as work songs.

Reciting poems in the classroom is another common but important way of experiencing poetry. The reciting may take place with or without preparation. It may take place spontaneously during a lesson when the pupil makes a connection with a known poem. It is then left to the teacher to seize this opportunity, to pause for a few minutes and reflect on the impression created by the poem.

An important part of the teacher's job is to help pupils become active listeners. The poetic word wants to be spoken out loud and listened to as a personal utterance, as a confession, a cry of sorrow or of joy. Such expressions can be considered as absolute ways of being alive, without reservations or barriers. They need to be read out loud, to be heard.

To recite a poem could be an inspirational introduction to a new theme or topic. It is a good way to begin the school day. Poems can be a new way of looking at a familiar theme. It is not difficult to find a poem suitable for almost every occasion and event. Because poems are vivifying fundamental experiences, they evoke basic questions and reactions. They are always closely connected with common situations in everyday life. Pupils need to be made aware of this and helped to make the connections.

Poetry is unique. No other type of text is so aware of language. This makes poetry ideal teaching material for language teachers. No other text experiments with language in the way that poetry does. As such it is a vital resource for language teachers. There are a number of ways in which teachers can develop the ideas already outlined. The teacher can introduce 'the poem of the day' or 'the poem of the week' as an idea to the pupils. Of course, in the initial stages the onus is on the teacher to initiate these ideas, but this can be done in the expectation that after a time the pupils will take over the responsibility for the choice and reciting of the poems. Pupils should be encouraged to introduce each poem with a short presentation. What is going on in the classroom meanwhile is an alert, active sort of listening. This can be encouraged if there is no printed copy of the text, no written word, no intellectual control of the words heard. The listeners' eyes should be closed or focused on something specific, perhaps the reciter. In this way, the outward and the inward ears are activated during this poetry reading activity. During the reading the sounds, the voice, the impression and imagination are the important phenomena. The poem is a certain voice, addressing the listener personally and urgently.

To prepare the pupils for these regular poetry readings and occasions, a collection of poetry books and anthologies needs to be displayed in the classroom, on a shelf or in a specific area of the library. Of course the pupils are allowed to ask for specific poems or suggest particular favourites, either anthologies or poets. Pupils' ideas should be taken into account when assembling the collection and selecting the books. The display should then be regarded as a communal resource available to all and used when searching for something specific. Pupils should be encouraged to use it when they are preparing for their own poetry reading and presentations. An introduction or warm-up session for the poem of the day activity could centre around a discussion of how to recite poems. A good starting point is the teacher's own reciting or reading of a particular poem. This can be recorded and listened to over and over again.

An alternative approach to this activity is to hand out to each pupil, at the beginning of the reading, their own copy of the poem as a printed text. Everybody in the class is then asked to read the text carefully. Pupils are asked how they would recite the text if they were doing the reading and to mark their text with cues in their own way. This should include a variety of aspects that help with the reading aloud or recitation, such as intonation, pronunciation, stress, pause, tone, and change of tone to create mood, pace, change of pace. Not all of these need to be addressed by each pupil. At this point, when everyone has had the opportunity to reflect on their interpretation of the poem, the texts and the comments and markings are removed from sight. It is now time for the teacher's recital. Again this can be tape-recorded. After the reading the pupils go back to their texts and listen to the reading again on the tape-recording. They then compare the teacher's reading with their own suggestions. In pairs, the pupils are encouraged to talk about the differences between their own ideas for reading the text and to compare them with the teacher's way of doing it. Impressions and opinions are then shared with the whole class. Similarities and differences of interpretation provide a focal point for discussing the text in more detail. There are a number of benefits to this approach to teaching poetry. It serves a variety of purposes, helping to throw light on the fact that:

- every recital is a unique way of understanding and interpreting the poem
- more understandings and varying interpretations of each poem are possible
- some understandings and interpretations are better than others, perhaps because they utilize better what the poem contains or because they give a greater experience or clearer sensation to the poem
- the poem is a voice that wants to be heard; it is an experience that can be transmitted physically to a wider audience
- an exchange of possibilities is taking place during our listening to the poem; this carries meaning to the listeners, who for their part provide the poem with meaning and coherence
- every poem has a certain shape, body or structure; it also has a personal appeal to the co-operating imagination, which emanates from past and present experiences seeking poetic understanding.

The tape-recorder is a useful teaching aid for encouraging active listening during poetry recitals. Pupils can also make use of the tape-recorder for teaching each other. In addition, it is an easy way to introduce the voice of the poet into the classroom. It may be possible to collect poets reading their own work from radio or television broadcasts. Some poets are also available on commercial recordings of their work, produced specifically for this purpose.

Once poetry has been introduced to the class in this way, it is possible to develop more specific activities. For example, rhythmic movement to poetry can be developed as a chain dance. Ballads are particularly suitable for this activity. The dance starts with two steps to the right and then one or two steps to the left. These simple movements are then repeated to the rhythm of the poem with one movement on each stressed syllable marking the beat. This is an excellent way of making clear what rhythm means.

Pupils can respond with physical movement both to poems that they are listening to and to poems they are reciting. These movements and gestures can also be accompanied by music that has been specially selected to match the poem. Groups of children can be asked to perform or illustrate their chosen poem in this way. Almost every poem that represents a progression, either inward or outward, is suitable for this activity. One suitable example is the second poem quoted at the beginning of this chapter.

After this type of preliminary activity we can eventually and slowly get round to *looking at* poems. One suggestion is to give each pupil in the group a book of poems to look at. They are also given, at the same time, another book written in prose and are set the task of comparing the two books. No close reading of the content is required. They are asked to form a more or less spontaneous impression of the two different books, in comparison with each other. Some points for guidance might include: How is the text arranged and placed? How is it grouped in the two different books? How is it composed? What are the main traits of the poetry book? Pupils' impressions do of course vary, but there will be some shared perceptions. The following pupils' remarks are not untypical. One said, 'The poetry book consists of many small parts, each of them having their own title and pages'; another said, 'The units are placed in the middle of the page(s) with lots of space around them.'

WAYS OF ACQUIRING POETIC KNOWLEDGE

Having set the scene for teaching poetry through the type of introductory activity already outlined, the next task is to help students to acquire some poetic knowledge. At this point the questions arise, what is significant about collections of poetry and what do they tell us about poems? It is at this time that the teacher may wish to capitalize on the opportunities offered by the various kinds of pupils' comments recorded above. For example, the teacher may want to suggest that poems are intended to be small, condensed moments of life and that that is the reason why they have so much space around them. The teacher may also go on to say that rhyme, rhythm, metre, figurative language, symbols and titles are signs, marking the poems as small entities and that these signs are recognized by the ear, the eye and, of course, the mind. To reinforce these points the teacher can hand out a small list outlining the main traits of a particular poem under discussion. The list should contain some of the familiar poetic characteristics of the poem. These points may include features such as contrast, repetition, variation, focus or a number of other poetic features.

What was developed earlier about poetic experience can now be combined with ways of acquiring poetic knowledge, using the teacher's list. Some of the songs, jointly sung in the classroom, may now be regarded as written poems. For example, when we examine the verses, the figurative language and the title of the text, its repetitions, variations and contrasts, we may find that poems and songs share some traits. However, we only pay attention to these details because we want to grasp and understand the poem as an entity, a small moment in life. On another day, at a different time, the focus may be somewhat different. For example, the search for poetic symbol within the text may be the dominant focus of the activity. Finding the symbol of the poem is an excellent way of interpreting it. The poetic symbol is the powerful centre of the poetic unit.

Using a tape-recording of one of the pupil's favourite songs may be the starting point for exploring the question of what makes this a poem. For this activity the pupils return to their lists, outlining the characteristics of the poem. They compare the list of characteristics with the traits of the song they have just listened to. They are asked to say which traits apply to the song. The class is then divided into small groups. Each group is asked to select just one characteristic trait for consideration. The song is then played again and the group tries to pick out as many examples as they can of their particular poetic trait. This may involve one group in listening for the figurative language of the song. They are then asked to give particular examples of their trait, and where in the song the trait appears. Pupils can be asked to say in what ways the traits are different and/or similar. This leads to the question of why are they all referred to as figurative language. What does this expression really mean? This becomes an opportunity to talk about features of the text.

Then the text of the song is distributed. Pupils are encouraged to comment on the differences between hearing the song and reading it as a poem. These differences become the focus of the twofold title of this chapter. They represent the two different ways of meeting a poem and illustrating a historical development. Reading the poem is rather a new way of enjoying poetry. It may interest the pupils to know that earlier presentations of poetry, for example the medieval ballad, took the form of a dance or song as an oral presentation.

At this point we can return to the rhymes and jingles that the pupils wrote down. They can be considered in the same ways as the songs. Pupils can be encouraged to look for traits and consider whether this collection of jingles can in some ways be considered a collection of poems. Individual jingles and poems can be compared, with particular attention paid to the sounds, the playing on words and the magic power of the words.

TWO POEMS AS EXAMPLES

At this point I should like to return to the two poems quoted earlier, and use them to illustrate other ways of helping pupils to acquire poetic knowledge. One way is to introduce the poem without the title. I did this at the beginning of the chapter:

> I wander chilly and bloodforsaken
> and snap at the sunset.
> Widescreen! Hollywood! Technicolor!
> And glare down at the flagstones
> stamped with greasy leaves
>
> Then a chestnut cracks at my feet.
> A bright brown eye opens.
> Behold heaven and earth
> for the first time.

It is now up to the pupils to suggest a possible title for the poem. This is an important activity because it requires a certain amount of understanding of what the poem is about, what it is trying to say, its theme, the most important words, the fundamental contrasts, its way of grasping at life and reacting to it. If the pupils can capture all of these points and suggest a title, then they have already understood a great deal about the poem. The pupils' suggestions are written on the blackboard. Each one is discussed in turn and the pupils consider what each reveals about the poem. We consider which one we prefer. Then at this point, it is time to introduce the Danish poet's own title, 'Widescreen'. (It was written by Benny Andersen in 1975 and translated by Alexander Taylor.[1]

We then compare our own ideas with Benny Andersen's original title and suggest the reasons behind his choice. In particular, the ambiguity of his title is noted. We note the headline, at first seeming to dislike it until it is understood as the artificial picture of the cinema screen. Later this dislike turns to wonder at the astonishing, unknown world that has a new-born existence.

There is another phenomenon which is rather important in Benny Andersen's poem; it is worth exploring in order to help the pupils to acquire poetic knowledge. We draw attention to the fact that the poem is divided into two sections, with space between them. Why is the poem constructed in this way? Could it have been done differently? What does the order of the two sections tell us about what is going on, about the progress and the attitude of the poem? We consider why we use the term 'sections' instead of verses. All of this discussion helps pupils to acquire a greater understanding and knowledge of poetry.

Acquiring poetic knowledge calls for pupil curiosity and active participation. I should like to outline another activity based on this poem. This time the pupils are given just two lines of the poem, the second line: 'Widescreen! Hollywood! Technicolor!' and the very last line 'for the first time'. With just these two lines the pupils are asked to say what they think is going on in the poem and to write down cue words. They then try to reconstruct the poem, line by line, each line growing out of the pupil's own cue words. This works well as a group activity, with the children inspiring each other and each offering ideas. What is produced has to be examined by its creators and the pupils are asked to reflect on their lines. Are they satisfied with the new lines and the final result? Once this discussion is over, Benny Andersen's original poem is revealed. Are they surprised? What are the differences between the various versions that have been created? Are we satisfied with the lines of the original poem? What comments are made about the progression?

Now, I should like to suggest yet another activity using this poem. The pupils are asked to tell a very short story based on a small amount of information. They are told that the story should be about a person (they can use 'I', 'she', or 'he') walking in the street. They are also given the following information: it is autumn and late in the afternoon; a chestnut falls down from a tree. Tell a story about the walk. It is important to keep the stories quite short for this activity. When everyone has composed a story, Benny Andersen's poem is handed out, together with the following questions: What does the poem tell? Is it a story? Why has the poet not chosen the title 'The Walk' for his poem?

These last two activities are recommended if, as a teacher, you want to appeal to the pupils' own imagination when you are helping them to recognize different ways of poetic expression. Another approach would be to hand out copies of Benny Andersen's poem without any comments or discussion at all. Ask the pupils to illustrate it. The individual drawings will show how the pupils have conceived and interpreted the poem,s and these different interpretations can be discussed afterwards.

Finally, I should like to make some suggestions for using the other poem quoted at the beginning of this chapter, in the classroom.

> I dwell in Possibility –
> A fairer House than Prose –
> More numerous of Windows –
> Superior – for Doors – 2

Pupils are asked to comment on anything which they find *strange* about this poem. Their impressions are used as the starting point for understanding the poem. Leading questions are posed to focus attention on particular aspects of the poem. For example, why do all these solemn words occur in this poem? Why is there a constellation of unequal phenomena, words from different areas of life? Why is the punctuation unusual, consisting only of dashes? These questions guide us through the poem in a number of ways:

- as a particular expression of mood and attitude
- as a spontaneous stream of imaginings, evoked by a certain thought or word ('possibility')
- as a way of talking that invites the receivers to be creative co-operators
- as figurative language that brings together different phenomena, divided parts of existence, in order to make our world and our imagination wider
- as a symbol which is concrete but also means more than that, pointing beyond itself.

This poem was in fact written by Emily Dickinson.

We perhaps begin to find out more about what this poem means when we try to give it a title. Perhaps it should be called 'Poetry', if the title is to represent what the poem is about.

NOTES

1. Andersen, Benny (1975) *Selected Poems* (translated by Alexander Taylor). Princeton: Princeton University Press.
2. This poem was written by Emily Dickinson. She has not given her poem a title. It was not published until after her death. According to Thomas H. Johnson's edition (*The Poems of Emily Dickinson*, 3 vols., published in 1955) the quoted lines are the first part of 'Poem 657'.

Chapter 5

Poetry Teaching in the Secondary School: The Concept of 'Difficulty'

Mike Fleming

INTRODUCTION

Despite what has been described as an 'explosion of interest in poetry in schools' in the 1980s (Merrick, 1991), writers on poetry continue to bear witness to its neglect and unpopularity in many classrooms. Research in the early part of the decade (APU, 1982) painted a bleak picture of the state of poetry teaching, but it is difficult to assess whether in more recent years the situation has improved. Such has been the energetic sharing of teaching ideas and the proliferation of new anthologies that it is likely that there has been some improvement. Wade and Sidaway (1990) summarize research findings and describe the results of their own study which reaffirmed teachers' lack of confidence in working with poetry. Atkinson's comment (1991) that 'poetry is one area of the English programme which continues to present problems' is not untypical.

In my own research on pupils' perceptions of poetry (which at the time was not specifically concerned with the notion of 'difficulty') I was struck by the number of pupils who claimed that they found poetry difficult and that this in part was a source of their antipathy to it. Why is this so and what are the implications for teachers and the teaching of poetry? In some ways it is surprising to learn that pupils find poetry difficult, because their earliest experiences of language constitute a delight in sounds, repetitions, rhythms and images without a narrow obsession with function and logic. It would be an unusual child who enquired how it was that the cow in the nursery rhyme managed to gain sufficient height to actually reach the moon or how, in the case of the little dog, it is possible to distinguish a laugh from a bark. Reeves (1965) in his *Understanding Poetry*, devoted one chapter to the poetic appeal of nursery rhymes because of his belief that they are an important foundation for the reader of poetry. Poetry, because it so often comprises language at its most charged and aesthetically appealing, and because of its associations with ritual, could be said to be the most 'natural' form of language. Why then does it pose problems as its readers become older? As pupils move from primary to secondary school there tends to be a growing emphasis on content and understanding, on *studying* as opposed to *experiencing* poetry. It is important to ask whether this transition accounts for pupils' negative reactions and whether the difficulty pupils find with poetry is not so much a property of the texts themselves but a function of the way schools teach poetry (Touponce, 1990).

TYPES OF DIFFICULTY

Steiner's classification (1978) of four types of difficulty provides a useful starting point for an exploration of the concept and its implications for the teaching of poetry. At a fairly straightforward level, some texts present difficulties to the reader because of the presence of obscure or archaic words, expressions or allusions (Steiner uses the term 'contingent' for this category). 'In the overwhelming majority of cases, what we mean by saying "this is difficult" signifies "this is a word, a phrase or a reference I will have to look up."' (Steiner, 1978: 27). Thus in Vernon Scannell's 'The Fair' words such as 'fusillades', 'pungent', 'feigned fever', 'lapped' might present young readers with difficulties. That is not to say, of course, that full comprehension of all contingent difficulties is necessary for enjoyment of the poem nor that understanding the meaning of unknown words will guarantee that the poem will be any more accessible. In the example given, the teacher might well decide that asking pupils to deduce lexical meaning from context is an appropriate and engaging exercise. On the other hand the accumulation of words such as 'latched', 'postern' and 'tremulous' in the first line of Hardy's 'Afterwards' might be enough to alienate the young reader from what is generally an accessible poem. In addition to the lexical and syntactical difficulties, the lack of knowledge of the allusions within a text or the absence of certain historical or contextual details may constitute a barrier to understanding. Much literary theory has tended to marginalize the importance of history in relation to texts, but lack of significant knowledge can present barriers. How, one might ask, can a reader understand Yeats' 'Easter 1916' without some knowledge of the political and historical events which are described in the poem?

> History functions as a factor in all literary theory, whether by its explicit incorporation into the theoretical framework, or by its attempted exclusion. And, though much may be made of texts as transcending history, as speaking to readers of all times, the literary work takes as its existence, first, within the history of the author's life, and, second, within the culture and its history. (Buchbinder, 1991: 99).

One of the decisions which the teacher has to make pertains to the appropriate lexical, syntactical, contextual or historical details which need to be supplied in order to provide enough clarity for the reader to be able to make an authentic response. Traditional approaches to poetry teaching based on inductive question and answer sessions and teacher explication would have no problem with this. Although the route might be circuitous, the eventual destination would be an accepted reading of the text. Richards' celebrated list of the ten principal difficulties encountered in poems, while still providing useful insights today, is based on the notion that reading a poem is a process of coming to know the text as object (Richards, 1929). Contemporary writers on poetry teaching such as Benton (1988), Dias and Hayhoe (1988), influenced by the theories of Iser and Rosenblatt, have stressed the constitutive role of the reader in the creation of meaning. The effect of reader-response theorists on practice has been to encourage teachers to intervene less in the way pupils respond to poems. The modern poetry classroom is more likely to see groups of pupils engaged in discussion in order to come to terms with texts for themselves, rather than being directed by the teacher. My own observation of classrooms leads me to suspect that some teachers have taken the non-intervention orthodoxy to an extreme, leaving pupils to struggle with poems without minimal and perhaps necessary guidance on particular aspects of the text. The balance is a delicate one because it is important not to convey a tacit message that the pupils' task is merely to uncover the poem's 'objective' and 'correct' meaning; it is important not to encourage the attitude that reading poetry is akin to problem solving:

> The major misconception of traditional teaching methodology is that far too often it implies that poems are puzzles to which the teacher holds the key, so that what have become emphasised in classroom discussion are the relative weaknesses of the children's readings and the paucity and inadequacy of their responses.
> (Benton *et al.* 1988: 2)

Steiner calls his second order of difficulty 'modal'. Here, clarity is not gained simply by looking words up or having the obscurities explained, because the problem derives from a failure to fully 'grasp' what the poem is about at a deeper feeling and aesthetic level. 'There is, at empirical levels, "understanding" – of the rough and ready order represented by paraphrase – but no genuine "comprehension", no in-gathering in the range of senses inseparable from the archaic Greek *legein* (to "assemble", to "enfold in meaningful shape")' (p. 28). Again, there are implications for the teacher's choice of poem and classroom methodology. My observations here are based on work with public secondary school coursework examinations in which teachers have control over the choice of poems. There has been a tendency for teachers to restrict their choice of poems to subject matter which seems likely to have immediate appeal to young people, so that bullying, fighting and other such themes are common. This is very understandable, because there is little more depressing for a teacher than to have pupils claim that poetry is boring. However, there is a danger that the pupil's diet of poetry in secondary school will become restricted to immediately accessible poems with predictable subject matter and a few 'contingent' difficulties.

Again the teacher is faced with a dilemma and the necessity of striking an appropriate balance between restricting choice of poetry texts to those which have immediate appeal or extending the canon and risking alienating pupils from the genre. Of course the way particular texts are introduced is an important factor in determining the way pupils respond. A recent anthology of poetry (Wood, 1988) introduces most poems with a preamble aimed at engaging pupils with the emotional territory of the poem. Thus Heaney's 'Death of a Naturalist' included the following questions as part of its introduction, 'What do we mean when we describe the child as "innocent"? What do you understand by the term "experience"? Have there been particular moments, particular experiences in your life after which you were never the same again?' For the same reason poems are often introduced within a theme, a technique which, while helping to contextualize the poem, runs the risk of circumscribing its meaning and reducing attention to the poem as a poem.

Steiner's *tactical* and *ontological* categories have similarities in that they both deal with difficulties which attach to poetry as a particular genre. The former arise because of the poet's deliberate concern to revitalize language as an intentional technique; grammatical and lexical difficulties arise because of the poet's concern to employ unique and unusual forms. It is the poet's aim to recharge language which has become worn and clichéd, to bring it new intensity and genuineness of feeling. Ontological difficulties arise in the poetry of the modern movement which challenged previous notions of what poetry is and how it should mean. Steiner's discussion of this category of difficulty is accompanied by an examination of the rise of modernism, which at its most extreme used private symbols and adopted complex new forms and styles. The challenge to the reader is to infer meaning from a minimum of highly condensed content. Reading poetry from the modern movement is a different matter from reading a Shakespeare sonnet. Steiner gives a historical explanation of the rise of modernism (in part a reaction to the 'philistine postivism of the industrial and mercantile structure of the nineteenth century', p. 41) but for the purposes of this paper it is enough to recognize that expectations of what poetry should mean and how it should function have changed over time, an insight which has implications for the teaching of poetry. The works of Donne, Eliot, Hughes, Raine and others may require different approaches in the classroom.

THE CONCEPT OF DIFFICULTY

What is apparent from Steiner's exploration of the concept is that questions about difficulty are tied up with questions about meaning and intention. When we employ the word 'difficult' in the context of communication we usually mean that some barrier exists which makes the process whereby information is transferred less transparent and denies access to the author's intended meaning. The removal of the barrier brings the necessary clarity. As indicated earlier, implicit in this view is a set of assumptions about the determinacy and stability of meaning. An alternative view would see the problem of difficulty residing in the reader's reluctance or inability to participate in the creation of meaning. The assumption of active readers is that

> they will ask questions and explore what a poem might be in the process of generating as an overall but provisional 'meaning'; that they will engage in 'intelligent guessing'; that they will cope with and even enjoy the problematic nature of the text, with its hints and clues and silences; that they will bring their life experiences with them to the text and be prepared to engage in sharing them and, sometimes, furthering them through discussion and scholarship, in order to engage more fully with the poem.
> (Dias and Hayhoe, 1988: 86)

It is also important to note that the term 'difficulty' in relation to poetry usually places the focus on content rather than form; it is an ability to determine what the poet is 'trying to say' which often leads to the judgement that a particular text is 'difficult'. 'The presupposition of difficulty arises from the combination of assumptions: first that the language of poetry is itself difficult, and, second, that there is concealed somewhere in this difficult language a "message" that is invisible to the naked eye' (Buchbinder, 1991: 1). The experience of being taught poetry can provide 'the irritating and debilitating feeling of being left out, of hearing the story but not getting the joke, or worse still, of then having to have the joke laboriously explained by a commentary' (Murray, 1989: 4).

Examination of our everyday use of the term also reveals that to say something is 'difficult' presupposes some understanding or participation in a shared context or 'form of life' (Wittgenstein, 1953). If I am handed a letter written in Spanish I am unlikely to say that it is difficult unless I can actually speak some Spanish. If I am completely ignorant of the language, the question of the difficulty of the letter is hardly relevant. I think this is important because when pupils identify poetry (as opposed to a particular poem) as being 'difficult' we need to unpack what is meant by that statement. What they may mean is that they find it bewildering or simply that it does not yield meaning in the same way as prose.

It might be helpful to illustrate some of the problems associated with the concept by looking at a specific poem, one by the American writer William Carlos Williams:

> This Is Just To Say
>
> I have eaten
> the plums
> that were in
> the icebox
> and which
> you were probably
> saving
> for breakfast
>
> Forgive me
> they were delicious
> so sweet
> and so cold.

What is interesting about this text is that there appears to be an absence of what would traditionally be judged as defining features of poetry: there is no figurative language or condensed meaning, nor is there an elaborate use of form and style. Would we describe this as a 'difficult' or 'easy' poem, or indeed as a poem at all? What is immediately striking is its simplicity, not just in the absence of metaphor but in the lack of any contextual detail. The simplicity and minimalist treatment underline an ambiguity of tone. Critical comment on the poem has, as one might expect, varied. An anthology for schools in which it appears explains, 'Williams is a poet of very positive attitudes, a celebrant of the joys of everyday living; I have included his tiny poem "This Is Just To Say" as a token example of this' (Wain, 1963). Elsewhere the poem is described as being 'much more than it seems: a celebration of the physical life, rendered with stringent economy but with a high degree of essential vividness' (Doyle, 1982: 55). Another critic sees it as a love poem, 'Love is to him something communicable in terms of the plums that were in the ice-box' (Larsson, 1935). The following comment is quoted anonymously in a collection of criticism as an example of how an ingenious and subtle critic can discover complexity and unity in almost anything:

> The irony of this poem was that precisely that which preserved them (the plums) and increased the deliciousness of their perfection (the refrigeration) contained in its essence the sensuous quality most closely associated with death: coldness. So the plums' death (or formal disappearance and disintegration) was symbolically anticipated in the charm of their living flesh. (Spears, 1980: 218)

From the point of view of this discussion of difficulty, the poem is interesting because of the absence of Steiner's categories of difficulty as a barrier to understanding. There are no contingent difficulties (the vocabulary and syntax could hardly be easier) nor do there appear to be any deliberate obscurities. It is less certain whether the 'modal' category applies; eating plums and writing a note are all within most people's experience but we could say that modal difficulties exist inasmuch as the reader may not be able to see any purpose or justification for what is written. The comments on the poem may not all strike a chord but warn against dismissing the work as trivial or meaningless.

Paradoxically, there is an argument for saying that the pupil who sees no difficulty at all in this poem is the naïve reader because the very way the words are set down on the page (as poem) invites us to speculate about its content and indeed its simplicity. Its simplicity is exactly what is problematic. The implicit theory of poetry held by the reader will probably be a factor in determining response. What this poem does is raise questions about the defining characteristics of the genre which could usefully be addressed in the classroom. For example, it might be interesting to compare the poem with the same text written in note form and pose the question:'To what degree does the change in presentation on the page change our reading of the text?'

THE TEACHING OF POETRY

What are the implications of this exploration of the concept of 'difficulty' for the teaching of poetry? Many writers have emphasized the importance of experiencing poems fully as opposed to a premature emphasis on analysis. Various classroom techniques such as recitals, drawings and dramatization are important, amongst other reasons, because they familiarize pupils with the texts in a non-threatening way without urging them to judgements. Benton (1988) has pointed out how readers come to terms with poems over time. If pupils approach poetry with the expectation that it will necessarily yield meaning in the way that much prose does, it is little wonder that it gets dismissed as being 'too difficult'.

At secondary level, becoming familiar with poems as opposed to merely trying to understand them is a necessary but not sufficient part of the poetry curriculum. It is not simply the demands of examinations which necessitate a closer study of form and content; the experience of poetry is likely to be enhanced by a closer exploration of meaning and effect. Teachers, however, need to find a balance between circumscribing pupils' responses by virtually telling them what to think, and leaving them bewildered and frustrated by their own inability to make sense of the text before them. It is after all possible to be wrong about certain aspects of particular poems. Roger McGough's 'Identification' is frequently read in secondary school and takes as its subject matter the identification of the body of a dead child by his father. Pupils left on their own to explore the poem do not always make that initial step of identifying what it is about. It is not enough to claim that their subjective response is valid and eschew the sort of objectivist position implied by the judgement that their initial reading is 'wrong', because the pupils themselves, and this is the crucial point, are likely to change their views after further exploration.

The important pedagogical point is to reject the elevation of any one methodology and recognize the necessity of treating particular poems in the classroom differently according to their different demands. I do not think this point is generally sufficiently acknowledged. Some texts lend themselves to unaided exploratory group discussion but not all do, and the appropriate choice is important in determining long-term attitudes to the genre as a whole.

If pupils find poetry bewildering (which I have suggested is often a more appropriate term than 'difficult'), they may be helped by some attention to the concept of poetry itself. I would not want to suggest that pupils require a course in poetics but that as they grow older they are capable of addressing questions to do with the nature of poetry in the context of comparisons with other types of language: thus advertising jingles, song lyrics, raps, traditional poems and verses all have a place in the poetry classroom.

REFERENCES

Assessment of Performance Unit (APU) (1982) *Language Performance in School: Secondary Survey Report No. 1.* London: HMSO.
Atkinson, J. (1991) How children chose poems. *Westminster Studies in Education,* **14**, pp. 57–67.
Benton, M., Teasey, J., Bell, R. and Hurst, K. (1988) *Young Readers Responding to Poems.* London: Routledge.
Buchbinder, D. (1991) *Contemporary Literary Theory and the Reading of Poetry.* Basingstoke: Macmillan.
Dias, P. and Hayhoe, M. (1988) *Developing Response to Poetry.* Milton Keynes: Open University Press.
Doyle, C. (1980) *William Carlos Williams: The Critical Heritage.* London: Routledge and Kegan Paul.
Fleming, M. (1992) Pupils' perception of the nature of poetry. *Cambridge Journal of Education,* **22** (1), pp. 31–41.
Larrson, R. (1935) Review, *Commonweal.* January, pp. 138–139. Reprinted in C. Doyle, (ed.) *William Carlos Williams: The Critical Heritage.* London: Routledge and Kegan Paul.
Merrick, B. (1991) The poetry explosion. *Children's Literature in Education,* **22** (1), pp. 25–34.
Murray, D. (ed.) (1989) *Literary Theory and Poetry – Extending the Canon.* London: Batsford.
Reeves, J. (1965) *Understanding Poetry.* London: Heinemann.
Richards, I. A. (1926) *The Principles of Literary Criticism.* London: Kegan Paul.
Spears, M. K. (1980) Imitative form and the failure of language. In C. Doyle, (ed.) *William Carlos Williams: The Critical Heritage.* London: Routledge and Kegan Paul.
Steiner, G. (1978) *On Difficulty and Other Essays.* Oxford: Oxford University Press.
Terrell, C. F. (ed.) (1983) *William Carlos Williams: Man and Poet.* Orono, Maine: National Poetry Foundation and University of Maine.
Touponce, W. (1990) *Literary Theory and the Notion of Difficulty.* New York: Centre for the Learning and Teaching of Literature.
Wade, B. and Sidaway, S. (1990) Poetry in the curriculum: a crisis of confidence. *Educational Studies,* **16** (1), pp. 75–84.
Wain, J. (1963) *Anthology of Modern Poetry.* London: Hutchinson.
Wittgenstein, L. (1953) *Philosophical Investigations* (translated by G. E. M. Anscombe). Oxford: Blackwell.
Wood, J. and Wood, L. (1988) *Cambridge Poetry Workshop.* Cambridge: Cambridge University Press.

Chapter 6

Creative Writing in Foreign Language Teaching
Carol Morgan

INTRODUCTION

The 'creative writing' referred to in the title means specifically the writing of poetry or poem-like creations in the context of teaching foreign languages, both in England and in other countries. In the analysis presented, I look at attitudes towards both poetry writing and poetry reading.

THE SUBJECT CONTEXT OF CREATIVE WRITING

There are three different contexts in Britain for looking at the writing of poetry in the classroom. These are: the teaching of English, the teaching of English as a foreign language (EFL) and the teaching of foreign languages (FL). Each context emphasizes different priorities and has different patterns of practice. In English language teaching, poetry writing and appreciation are recognized as an integral part of the syllabus. In Benton's (1986: 15) survey of 175 teachers in primary and secondary schools, for example, 47 per cent rated reading and discussion of poems as very important and 32 per cent put the writing of poetry in this category. In EFL teaching, literature and poetry have featured recently as a new focus, with primary and secondary sources spawning a crop of literature-cum-language books.[1] Here, however, the focus is generally on the use of literary texts for a variety of general language-based activities. In FL teaching little has been written. A few articles have appeared on the teaching of literature and poetry.[2] A-level syllabuses have always offered literature as an option for study (and this option is still preferred by schools in boards which offer literature and coursework/topics),[3] but poetry is only rarely included in the range of texts.[4] In the pre-sixteen syllabus poems or songs surface occasionally in textbooks, but the primary teaching focus is on functional communicative language work relating to the everyday world of the pupil and people in foreign countries. Some recognition of the deficiencies of this focus is evident from the inclusion of a new area of study in the National Curriculum regulations for Key Stages 3 and 4: 'The World of Imagination and Creativity'.[5] Elsewhere very little or no mention is made of the possibility of creative writing in the language being studied. One notable exception is the evidence of work carried out in Cambridgeshire as the result of two creative writing projects. The County Council has produced two collections of poetry in French, German, Spanish and Urdu written by students in the county.[6] There has also been some interest recently in Germany in the area of creative writing. One complete issue of the journal *Der Fremdsprachliche Unterricht* was devoted to creative writing in French (vol. 3, August 1991) and work by Michael Legutke and others has explored the possibilities of the interactive learning and teaching of English with poetry.[7] The approach here moves beyond simply viewing poetry as a catalyst for communication in the foreign language and values creative writing in its own right.

THE CLASSROOM CONTEXT

There is, then, a varied background to the teaching of creative writing and the writing of poetry, with foreign language teaching running a very poor third. An examination of the aims, classroom context and audience in the three different teaching areas identified here will help to identify the differences and possibly useful interchanges between these areas. It could suggest to foreign language teachers methods and approaches which could be useful in meeting the new demands of the National Curriculum, should they feel that their teaching currently lacks a creative element.

In the teaching of English and foreign languages the teaching context is generally the same: the school classroom with pupils aged 11–18 years, with these subjects also offered to adults at other educational establishments. English is also taught in primary schools, and research and materials here can be useful in thinking about possible approaches for foreign language teaching at a primary level. The attitude of secondary pupils towards poetry, identified by the APU survey in 1982[8] would seem a useful source of information for teachers intending to teach creative writing in both subject areas. The survey reveals what one already suspects from classroom practice, that 11-year-olds are more interested in poetry than 15-year-olds and that girls are more interested than boys.[9] The nadir appears to be a fourth year class of adolescent boys. Figures here are given for reading poetry, but one can perhaps expect similar attitudes to writing poetry. As some of the same pupils would have been attending English and foreign language classes these factors would appear to have the same relevance for teachers of both subjects.

However, different linguistic contexts will be working for the pupils in the two different subjects. For the pupil in the English classroom, several registers of English language will operate: the English he or she speaks with his or her peers and family, the English of the media (television, magazine, comics, books) that he or she reads, and the English of the classroom. These registers may or may not cohere or coincide. Attitudes of English teachers vary as to the accommodation of these different registers. Some, like Jill Pirrie, seek to shift their pupils into a higher linguistic gear through the use of literary models: 'through a literary experience, their [the pupils'] own ordinary lives have been heightened' and, in talking of using a Prévert model, 'Jacques Prévert has provided them with a framework for their own perceptions and observations. Through receiving his voice, they find their own' (Pirrie, 1987: 2, 8). Certainly the stunning results of her own pupils in national poetry competitions bear witness to the effectiveness of this approach. They were awarded 25 per cent of the prizes for the entire country in the 1987 W. H. Smith's Young Writers Competition and have a consistent record of winners each year. Other practitioners opt for different registers. Michael Rosen, for example, values what he terms 'oral writing': 'I would validate the oral mode ... ways of writing things down that reflect the way we say things' (Rosen, 1989: 44). He rejects the notion of elevating or heightening language to a prescribed literary level: 'The best order, best words approach is to my mind fairly pointless because inevitably it starts from adult literary notions of what "best" means ... We need to find forms that release children's knowledge, liberate it and so give the child a sense of his or her own power' (Rosen, 1989: 44).

For both these teacher-theorists, even though their priorities are different, there is a recognition of possibly conflicting registers in the heads of their pupils. This is generally not the case for foreign language learners. Unless the pupil has resided abroad, the register they know is based on their classroom language. There is no conflict between a familiar register they are at ease with and a register of the same language which is privileged by the teacher. They know almost only the language and register which has been taught. For these pupils almost the opposite problem exists: they may have difficulty in conceiving the language as *anything other* than a tool for functional and informational purposes. They may see French, German, Spanish or Italian only as a language for buying a train-ticket, ordering a meal or writing a newspaper report. Creative writing can reveal a wider and richer spectrum of language use and convince pupils, as Hunfeld (1990: 28) puts it, that 'a foreign language has more to offer than just text-book sentences'.[10] Here then pupils may be able to accept the broadening of language use without having any personal conflict of registers.

A further difference worth noting here is that English taught as a foreign language in this country may often have an audience of adults, with a consequent lowering of possible hostility towards poetry. My own experience with adults, in two creative-writing sessions with German teachers of English (run at the Hessische Institut für Lehrerfortbildung at the Rheinhardswaldschule in Kassel, November 1990 and 1991), revealed uncertainty and lack of confidence in tackling something new rather than hostility to the notion of writing poetry.

A key benefit of creative writing identified by theorists and teachers is its personal nature. In Benton's survey, 'self-expression' was the most highly rated value in assessing creative writing (34 per cent) together with 'an outlet for feelings and emotions' (25 per cent) (Benton, 1986: 16). Quotations cited above from Pirrie and Rosen have targeted the personal: 'Through receiving [Prévert's] ... voice, they [the pupils] find their own'; 'forms ... release children's knowledge ... and give the child a sense of his or her own power'. The personal aspect of creative writing is particularly valuable in foreign language learning since much of what is learnt is transferred language from artificial situations. Pupils are given the opportunity to discuss their own experiences both orally and in written work (for example, describe your house, write a description of activities at your school for your pen-friend etc.), but they are rarely given the opportunity to fantasize or set their own agenda. Ingrid Mummert (1991: 5) describes her own French pupils' disappointment at the lack of personal involvement: 'Pupils have said to me again and again how bad they feel that so little of their own thinking appears in what they write in the foreign language.'[11]

Legutke (1985: 86) also comments on the value of this outlet for self-expression, believing this to be enhanced by the neutrality of the foreign language medium:

> Approaching poetry in such a way [word play, sentence play and writing of poetry] can have rewarding results on a variety of levels: ... Learners become aware of their own feelings and the feelings of fellow learners (we discovered that students find it much easier to express their feelings in a foreign language than in their mother tongue, thus it would seem that the target language provides a safety-net for learners to express their emotions).

One word of warning needs to be signalled here: this very opening-up of channels, which may be of benefit to pupils and increase pupil–teacher understanding, may also constitute an unexpectedly painful source of revelation. In the topics selected by the pupils involved in my own creative writing lessons, it is interesting to see the expression of the anxieties and desires of adolescent love and concern over pending global environmental and social disaster. The following three poems serve as illustrations (Figures 6.1, 6.2 and 6.3).

Mummert (1991: 10) comments too on the frequency of love as a topic in creative writing in FL teaching although it is not commonly found in the general run of language work: 'the tendency to write about love or being in love ... occurs very little in foreign language teaching but appears frequently in the writing of poetry'.[12] Creative writing thus privileges certain topics which may be beyond the scope of normal classroom intercourse and may, while valuably forming an outlet for these, also create its own tensions.

Two other benefits of creative writing deserve mention: the opportunity to display wit and the satisfaction of producing an aesthetically pleasing object. The first links more closely perhaps with the release and distance experienced in writing in a foreign language. Gisela Hermann (1990: 57–74) has noted that students more often express personal rather than conventional opinions when voicing them in a foreign language in her survey of ethnocentricity:[13] 'The foreign language form helps to dispel on a cognitive level those ideas which are usually [conventionally] present and thus leaves the way open for more personal reactions.'[14]

She suggests, then, a closer, less programmed interaction with the language which derives from its unfamiliarity (compare for example the freshness of clichés and idioms when encountered in a foreign language). Legutke's comments on easier expression of feelings in the target language, quoted above, are also pertinent here. The desire to be witty perhaps also stems from this free interaction with language and was certainly a feature of my own experiments.

This is also a part of the whole process of playing around with language from which poetry derives. Hayhoe and Parker (1988: 3) point particularly, for example, to 'children's (and others') delight in jokes and outrageous puns' in their delineation of the 'ordinary', non-arcane nature of poetry. Delight may also come from production and this is an area which is shared by writers of poems in both the mother-tongue and foreign languages. The encouragement of a school magazine, classroom wall display or national competition as a destination can provide an extra incentive for production. As one of Jill Pirrie's pupils puts it, when thinking about entering poems for the W. H. Smith competition and book, 'I think it makes you try harder at them so they will get into the book.' There was certainly a marked difference in morale in the bottom fourth year set (Year 10) of a girls' selected-entry independent school who took part in my first experiments in creative writing. Their perceptions of themselves as 'the thick group' were shifted into a more positive gear after seeing their poetic creations on display in class. Mummert too comments (1991: 10) on the pleasure experienced by students in producing an attractive finished object: 'pupils enjoy writing out [their poems] again, making a fine copy, in fact of making that copy fine or finer.'[15]

EXPERIMENTS IN CLASS

In my own attempts at teaching creative writing I concentrated on freedom: students were free to choose the subject of their poems, free to choose the form and free to work alone or with a partner. The only stipulation was that they should produce something in the target language which was attractive or interesting enough to display on the classroom wall. The objectives

Figure 6.1 *Poem by two 14-year-old English girls*

La Pomme

La pomme c'est ronde, comme le monde,
Et la pomme c'est vert,
Tristement le monde ce n'est plus vert.
La pluie coule sur la pomme
Et le monde pleure

Alex

Figure 6.2 *'La Pomme'* – a poem written by Alex, a 14-year-old English girl

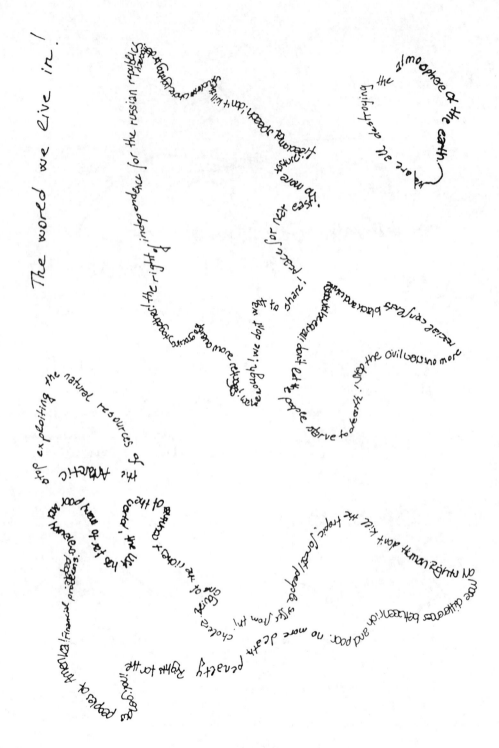

Figure 6.3 'The world we live in!' A poem by Beatrix and Anneke, two German students aged 18 years

here were to give the students an opportunity to use language in a different way and for them to produce a piece of language work which was valued rather than corrected (any problems of vocabulary or accuracy were dealt with during the drafting stages). Creative writing can be feared as anarchic, setting its own agenda. Benton (1986: 84) points to the misguided interpretations of 'progressive' creative work where 'self-expression meant anarchy or licence because pupils' work was "inspiration" and therefore sacrosanct'. It can also be feared in an FL context because the language of poetry may not follow standard grammatical rules. Legutke points to this fear amongst German teachers of English: 'In linguistic terms one could argue that poetry is a deviation from the norms of language ... Rather than improving language proficiency, working with poetry might be counterproductive to teaching the foreign language as a conventional system; at least this seems to be a widespread belief among [German] English teachers' (Legutke, 1985: 84). But it is this very deviation or freedom which can make poetry so attractive to the writer. Even a low-ability student can produce something attractive with a minimal range of vocabulary. A comment from one of Jill Pirrie's 13-year-old pupils is telling in this context: 'I like making poems spare. With prose you've really got to go into more detail.'

Students cannot, however, be expected to suddenly produce works of art, and some kind of help is vital from the teacher. Pirrie's method of providing literary models, detailed information on subjects, artists' drafts of poems and so on, focuses pupils' attention on new and extended ways of using language and ideas. My aim was to demystify poetry, to show that poems need not rhyme, could use simple language, or could combine a variety of visual elements to produce an attractive package. In my first experimental attempt with a fourth year French class of girls of average ability, I used a Prévert poem, 'Déjeuner du matin', read through quite quickly to show that poetry could be both accessible and enjoyable, and I then allowed pupils two lessons to produce a poem of their own making which incorporated some kind of pictorial element. In my later attempts with German students (15- and 18-year-olds in a mixed school) and with German teachers of English, I distributed examples of pupils' poems in English and a variety of 'shape' poems illustrating different techniques including concrete poems, acrostics and poems with pictures. In the German school these were one-off lessons so the process was truncated and the finished products were sent to me later. With the teachers as much time was allowed as they wished, with some teachers working late into the evening to produce a finished article acceptable to them. Tarleton's 1983 survey (quoted in Benton, 1986: 48) of children's perceptions of poetry focuses particularly on their response to form: 'These eleven year olds not only have a strong sense of form but they regard it as the most important feature of poetry.' Michael Benton *et al* (1988: 22–23) highlight the narrative and aesthetic functions of the poem with suggestions for positive responses to poems: 'Reading a poem is an event in time and an artefact in space ... we read a poem forwards ... we read a poem as a design.' Clearly the 'design' aspect of poetry provided a viable way into creative writing for the students in my groups.

FUTURE DEVELOPMENTS

In researching the area of creative writing and in my own experiments I have become aware of other different approaches which could be fruitful. Three of these deserve particular mention: the use of language exercises, the use of information technology (IT) and the use of music or art.

Language exercises

Language exercises linked to poetry are very much the province of the TEFL world. Joanne Collie and Stephen Slater's book, *Literature in the Language Classroom: A Resource Book of Ideas and Activities*, for example, provides some stimulating language work based on poems and Hunfeld (1990: 35–41) shows how simple grammar patterns can form the basis for poems. This seems a fruitful resource to explore and may help to overcome the fears of language teachers, cited above, that poetry will not teach 'proper' language. There seems no reason why language exercises based on vocabulary gathering or grammatical patterns should not also form the basis for the writing of poetry. Sandy Brownjohn in her two volumes of suggestions for stimulating creative writing *Does it have to Rhyme?* (1980) and *What Rhymes with Secret?* (1982), provides a variety of other preliminary language activities.

Information Technology

IT is a popular feature of many syllabuses and there can be several benefits in teaming up creative writing with the use of the computer. Firstly, the equipment lends itself to collaborative activity: pupils are used to working co-operatively on IT projects and could thus easily take on the building of a poetic text. Secondly, the computer allows for easy handling of a text with sections transposed quickly and alterations accommodated with no difficulty. Thirdly, the final product can be an attractive product which the student may take pride in. Hayhoe and Parker (1988: 91–92) point to the attraction of this mode of writing: 'Some children become highly motivated when using this medium for writing.'

Music and art

A variety of stimuli can be used to trigger creative writing. The most common is the reading of a poem on a subject, the discussion of it, followed by the writing of a poem on the same subject, a conventional process perhaps too well-tried, described by Peter Benton (1986: 21) as 'the three-box shape'. As shown above, a variety of other stimuli can also be effective. The notion of using music and/or art as catalysts is interesting in that they relate to the use of affect in language training. Suggestopedia has already capitalized on this and the use of classical music in accelerated learning utilizes the combination of affective and cognitive learning. Some experiments carried out by Alfons Knauth with German secondary pupils, using pictures by Miro and Matisse, produced a range of imaginative poems.[16] Matisse's 'Icare', for example, was interpreted in different ways – the central figure being either male or female and the different coloured features of the poem having related meaning – a joyful red heart, blue sky, yellow stars or a blood-red wound, a blue hell and yellow fires.

Here then the visual element provides the centre for the poem rather than supporting it as in the examples given above. Legutke (1991: 89) suggests music as a possible stimulus: 'Let students write poetry while listening to music. The poems can be a story dream, a description of a scene etc.' Maley and Duff (1990: 120–21) include the beat of particular musical pieces, the opening of Beethoven's 5th Symphony for example, as a possible schema for the rhythm of a poem. Here too there seem to be added benefits in a synaesthetic approach.

CONCLUSION

Perhaps some of the apprehension regarding the teaching and writing of poetry stems from anxiety about the nature of poetry itself. Benton (1986: 16) identified two different prevailing attitudes towards creative writing amongst the teachers who were interviewed in his survey: a belief that writing poetry was a source of pleasure for pupils on the one hand and on the other the feeling that 'children's natural antipathy to poetry, which they find alien, irrelevant and "posh", is strengthened by teachers who make too much of it by demanding a creativity which most pupils, particularly the less able, are quite incapable of achieving'. Rosen (1989: 10) avoids the problem to some extent by choosing the terminology 'Bits' and 'Stuff' for his own and his pupils' creations: 'I have been quite happy to leave the "is-it-poetry?" debate with people who need to worry about such things.' The criteria in the mind of the teacher will be influential in the response of the pupil. By taking 'creative writing' as my focus I hope to have shifted attention from the product – the acceptable poem – to the process – the enjoyment of a new way of writing.

NOTES

1. See for example: C. Brumfit and R. Carter, *Literature in Language Teaching* (Oxford: OUP, 1986); R. Carter and M. Long, *The Web of Words: Exploring literature through Language* (Cambridge: CUP, 1987); D. Clarke, *Talk about Literature* (London: Arnold, 1989); J. Collie and S. Slater, *Literature in the Language Classroom: A Resource Book of Ideas and Activities* (Cambridge: CUP, 1987); A. Duff and A. Maley, *Literature* (Oxford: OUP, 1990); J. Hill, *Using Literature in Language Teaching: Teaching Literature in the Language Classroom* (London: Macmillan, 1986); A. Maley and A. Duff, *The Inward Ear: Poetry in the Classroom* (Cambridge: CUP, 1989); A. Maley and S. Moulding, *Poem into Poem: Reading and Writing Poems with Students of English* (Cambridge: CUP, 1985).
2. For example, Ayse Akyer, 'The use of literature in content-based writing: a conceptual framework', *Language Learning Journal*, 1990, **2**, pp. 37–38; Gary Chambers, 'Suggested approaches to A-level literature', *Language Learning Journal*, 1991, **4**, pp. 5–9; D. Constantine, 'Encouraging an appreciation of poetry', in *German in the Classroom*, ed. A. Jones and K. Whitton (London: MLA, 1984).
3. The figures for JMB 1991 are 5,683 and 1,417 respectively and for London in the same year 4,096 and 524. It also needs to be noted that topics or coursework may in themselves also include literature, so the literature bias is in fact even higher.
4. Poems by Neruda, for example, appear in the Spanish A-level syllabus (London Syllabus A 1993/4) and poems by Prévert in the Oxford and Cambridge 1991 syllabus.
5. 'Area G' in the 'Areas of Experience', *Modern Foreign Languages in the National Curriculum*, (DES, London: HMSO, 1991), p. 29.
6. *A World of Words* (1989), *Another World of Words* (1991) Cambridge: Cambridgeshire County Council. They have also produced a handbook on creative writing in the FL classroom.
7. See Michael Legutke, 'Interactive approaches to poetry' in *Schüleraktivierende Methoden im Fremdsprachenunterricht Englisch* (Bochum: Kamp, 1985); Hans Hunfeld, *Literatur als Sprachlehre: Ansätze eines hermeneutisch orientierten Fremdsprachenunterrichts* (Berlin: Langenscheidt, 1990).
8. DES, *Language Performance in School: Secondary Survey Report No. 1* (HMSO, 1982).
9. 59 per cent of 11-year-olds agreed with the statement 'I like reading poetry' as against 32.4 per cent of 15-year-olds. 50 per cent of boys at 11 expressed positive views with 23.6 per cent at 15, set against 68.8 per cent of girls at 11, and 41.5 per cent at 15.
10. 'eine fremde Sprache mehr zu bieten hat, als Lehrbuchsätze' (Hunfeld, p.28, see Note 7).

11. 'Schüler/Innen haben mir immer wieder gesagt, wie peinlich es ihnen sei, dass so wenig von ihren Gedanken in der Fremdsprache, der von ihnen formulierten Antwort wirklich zum Ausdruck kommt' (Ingrid Mummert, 'Kreatives Schreiben im Fremdsprachenunterricht', *Der Fremdsprachliche Unterricht,* **3**, pp. 4–11, p. 5).
12. 'die Neigung... der Liebe oder Verliebtheit zu schreiben... ist im Fremdsprachenunterricht eine... seltene Erscheinung, beim Gedichteschreiben aber häufig zu entdecken' (Mummert, 1991, p. 10, see Note 11).
13. The survey was carried out with 17- and 18-year-old German pupils, proficient in English, with a questionnaire in English and German. 'L'influence de la langue étrangère sur la perception sociale et ethnique: étude interculturelle', *Langues Modernes*, **2** (1990), pp. 57–74.
14. 'La forme linguistique étrangère contribue apparemment à bannir du niveau cognitif les notions habituellement prévalentes et ouvre ainsi le chemin à des impulsions plus individuelles.'
15. 'Schüler/Innen die Texte... gern noch einmal "schön" abschreiben, ja verschönernd abschreiben' (Mummert, p. 10, see Note 11).
16. 'Carte postale poétique: Kreative Korrespondenz im Französischunterricht (Sek. II)', *Der Fremdsprachliche Unterricht*, **3**, 1991, pp. 33–37.

* An earlier version of this chapter appeared in *Language Learning Journal* (September 1994) under the title 'Creative writing in foreign language teaching'.

REFERENCES

Benton, M., Teasey, J., Bell, R. and Hurst, R. K. (1988) *Young Readers Responding to Poems*. London: Routledge.
Benton, P. (1986) *Pupil, Teacher, Poem*. London: Hodder and Stoughton.
Brownjohn, Sandy (1980) *Does it Have to Rhyme?* Sevenoaks: Hodder and Stoughton.
Brownjohn, Sandy (1982) *What Rhymes With Secret?* Sevenoaks: Hodder and Stoughton.
Collie, J. and Slater, S. (1987) *Literature in the Language Classroom: A Resource Book of Ideas and Activities*. Cambridge: CUP.
DES (1982) *Language Performance in School: Secondary Survey Report No. 1*. London: HMSO.
Duff, A. and Maley, A. (1989) *The Inward Ear: Poetry in the Classroom*. Cambridge: CUP.
Duff, A. and Maley, A. (1990) *Literature*. Oxford: OUP.
Hayhoe, M. and Parker, S. (1988) *Words Large as Apples: Teaching Poetry 11–18*. Cambridge: CUP.
Hermann, G. (1990) L'influence de la langue étrangère sur la perception sociale et ethnique: étude interculturelle. *Langues Modernes*, **2**, pp. 57–74.
Hunfeld, Hans (1990) *Literatur als Sprachlehre: Ansätze eines hermeneutisch orientierten Fremdsprachenunterrichts*. Berlin: Langenscheidt.
Knauth, A. (1991) Carte postale poétique: Kreative Korrespondenz im Französischunterricht (Sek. II) *Der Fremdsprachliche Unterricht*, **3**, pp. 33–37.
Legutke, Michael (1985) Interactive approaches to poetry. In *Schüleraktivierende Methoden im Fremdsprachenunterricht Englisch*. Bochum: Kamp.
Mummert, Ingrid (1991) Kreatives Schreiben im Fremdsprachenunterricht. *Der Fremdsprachliche Unterricht*, **3**, pp. 4–11.
Pirrie, Jill (1987) *On Common Ground: A Programme for Teaching Poetry*. London: Hodder and Stoughton.
Rosen, M. (1989) *Did I Hear You Write?* London: André Deutsch.
Tarleton, R. (1983) Children's thinking about poetry. *NATE News*, Summer 1983, quoted in Benton, p. 48.

Chapter 7

Teaching Poetry in the Secondary School in France
Jean-Marie Fournier

This study was carried out by a team of researchers at the French National Institute of Pedagogical Research (INRP) in Paris. It is an empirical description of the lists or corpus of texts that candidates have to study for the oral part of the French Literature *baccalauréat* (the final exam of secondary education in France). The texts on these lists are those studied in French schools during the school year prior to the study (1992). As such, they not only provide a representative sample of French secondary school examination work, but they also reflect the teachers' conception of the study of poetry as a discipline.

Before presenting the findings of the study, it is first necessary to give some background information about the material. The texts are selected for the exam in two ways. Some of them are extracts from complete works which have been read all the way through from beginning to end. In this case, the list of texts refers to these extracts and indicates the precise themes and literary problems that have been taught and dealt with in class. The other texts consist of assembled extracts which share a common theme, or materials that enable students to study a particular literary theme. One important theme, for example, is the question of aesthetics; another is the history of a genre. Each group of texts has a title indicating the reasons for its inclusion in a particular list.

These two kinds of texts constitute two different corpora. The former will be referred to as the *complete works corpus* and the latter as the *text groupings corpus*. The whole corpus contains 585 lists collected in different school districts (what are know as *academies* in France). They account for almost the whole of the country. The corpora are large enough to be significant, even though it was not possible to collect data to pre-stated criteria.

Outlined here is a description of the poetic corpus that has been read and studied at the end of secondary school education. First, however, I should like to present more information about the corpus itself. The corpus is in no way influenced by the French Ministry of Education. Teachers are free to study any text with their pupils that they consider relevant or sufficiently interesting from a literary point of view. Although some texts, or complete works, are recommended in official directives, they are in no way imposed upon teachers. This may account for the diverse nature of the corpus. Some works have been chosen because they are in line with the aims and objectives of the school system. A corpus assembled in this way has a kind of stability and consistency which, although not imposed, emerges as a system. The purpose of the INRP study was to investigate the coherence of the corpus, which represents what we could call 'school literature', or at least a school view of literature.

We begin with the following simple statement: at a very straightforward level, the corpus is organized according to two different parameters. They are genres such as poetry, drama, novels (or more generally speaking, narrative works) and philosophical prose, and texts that are historically representative of particular periods of French history. Textbooks used in class, for example, generally follow a historical structure based on the established periods in French literary history.

The questions we are trying to answer could be formulated more precisely as follows: If we say that poetry is a literary category, can we describe its function, its status, and the way in which knowledge about it is created in the school system from an epistemological point of view?

THE STATUS OF POETRY IN THE CORPUS

Reading a complete work at school, or having to deal just with an extract of the same work, are two completely different tasks. This is especially true of poetry. The way the texts are read differs and so do the pupils' expectations. For instance, it is possible to carry out systematic analyses of short extracts, but this is not feasible with longer extracts or complete works.

Tables 7.1 and 7.2 show the occurrence, in the corpus, of poetry from each century. Table 7.1 shows when the texts appear as complete works and Table 7.2 when they appear just as extracts.

Table 7.1 Poetry studied as complete works in French secondary schools

Century	Occurrences
16th	0
17th	2
18th	0
19th	90
20th	34

Table 7.2 Poetry studied as extracts

Century	Occurrences	Percentage
16th	174	6.4%
17th	125	4.6%
18th	14	0.5%
19th	1771	65.4%
20th	625	23.0%

In Table 7.2 the percentages represent the ratio between the extracts from poetic works and the total number of extracts from all genres including drama and the novels for each century. For example, the 174 occurrences for the sixteenth century represent 6.4 per cent of the literary texts read by the class.

The tables reveal two facts of particular interest. First, it is clear that poetry is usually read in school as extracts, rather than complete works. Second, poetry is chosen mainly from the works of the nineteenth and twentieth centuries. The significance of the number of nineteenth-century works has to be adjusted in the light of the fact that among the 90 occurrences recorded, no fewer than 69 can be accounted for by the choice of *Les Fleurs du mal* by Baudelaire.

It is clear from both tables that texts from the nineteenth and twentieth centuries dominate the choice of poetry studied in French secondary schools. There are other trends to note. As a consequence of the particular choice of texts studied in the secondary schools there are some gaps in the school literature syllabus. Because of the dominance of nineteenth- and twentieth-century texts, some of the key characteristics of poetry do not appear in the teaching of literature at school level in France. Most of the complete works studied at secondary school are novels or drama (plays). Poetry, in particular anthologies or complete collections of works, is scarcely taught.

The small amount of sixteenth-century poetry in the school curriculum raises an interesting question about poetry collections. What makes *Les Fleurs du mal* a good text for school study, while *Les Amours* of Ronsard or *Les Regrets* of du Bellay are not chosen? Language difficulties might offer a possible explanation. If this were the case, one would expect to find the same trend in other texts selected for study. However, this does not seem to be a constraint in the case of classical drama, which is well represented in the school curriculum.

The different structures of these collections are probably the key to the problem. *Les Fleurs du mal*, as a collection of poems, exhibits a thematic organization at different levels: section titles, sub-titles and poem titles. Thus a thematic reading can be justified, founded on features proposed by the author himself. On the other hand, poetry collections from the sixteenth century have a more linear structure; the majority of them are made up of a series (of sonnets, for example), and are variations on a poetic form. The complexity of such structures makes them less easy to approach in a thematic way.

This leads us to another, quite radical, question: What is a school text? From our survey findings, it is possible to observe two different types of school text. The first is the short text (or extract) and the second is a long one. The teachers' choice of a long, or unabridged work, depends upon certain constraints. This trend is clear when we look at Table 7.3. This shows an overview of the types of literary text, drama and narrative as well as poetry, that have been studied by secondary school pupils in French schools.

Table 7.3 *An overview of the texts studied in secondary schools in France*

Century	Theatre	Narrative Works	Poetry
16th	2 (50%)	1 (25%)	0 (0%)
17th	19 (82.6%)	2 (8.7%)	1 (4.3%)
18th	7 (31.8%)	13 (59%)	0 (0%)
19th	6 (9.1%)	49 (74.2%)	11 (16.6%)
20th	30 (22%)	83 (61%)	13 (1%)

These works studied at secondary school level appear to be identified by two different features: the literary genre which they represent and the century in which they were written. Thus the seventeenth century, for example, was mainly a century of theatre, the nineteenth a century of poetry and the novel. The case of the eighteenth century is different in some ways. French schools appear to define this century in a negative way. It is not clearly characterized according to the formal criteria we have used so far. The eighteenth-century corpus is not formally but thematically coherent. From the lists, we see that this century is mainly studied for different reasons, as a philosophical study, the century of the Enlightenment.

We can conclude from the formal data that the historical development of literary forms is not a teaching topic, and is not relevant, generally speaking, to literary studies at the secondary school level. The combined historical and formal classifications allocate a literary genre to one of its historical stages, considered the best or the most typical and connected in each case to a particular movement. Poetry, for example, at the end of secondary education, is chosen from the romantic or post-romantic periods.

NINETEENTH-CENTURY POETRY: READING BAUDELAIRE

The reading lists that we gathered do not represent the full range of literature studied within the school curriculum. They are merely one aspect of it. Given this kind of data, it is impossible, of course, to say exactly what reading a complete work in a secondary class actually means. Nonetheless, the choice of *Les Fleurs du mal* by a number of teachers gives some information about the way a long poetic text is treated.

Les Fleurs du mal as a school text

A statistical investigation of the texts chosen in Baudelaire's work reveals a disparity between the different pieces. Some of them constitute what we could call the school edition of *Les Fleurs du mal*, which is not the complete collection. This imposes limitations.

The poems chosen are generally those of the 1861 edition. This means that the condemned poems remain in the background and are not prominent. This systematic omission is hardly just a matter of chance. It seems that the weight of the old censure and some literary phobias are still to be found in today's schools. Among the non-censured poems of the first edition which never appear in the school lists are, for example, Sonnet 33, 'Une nuit que j'étais près d'une affreuse juive', and Sonnet 25 in which Baudelaire flies from the impure woman.

We can also observe that there is nothing in the lists to draw attention to the trial against Baudelaire and his book. In only one list could we find any reference to the important connection in Baudelaire's work between beauty and evil. There is never any problematic approach to Baudelaire's poetry based on the relationship between the poet and the society of his time, as exhibited in the *Fleurs du mal* trial and the text itself. These seem to be entirely omitted from the school lists.

More generally, even if we only consider the text of the 1861 edition, we observe that 35 of these poems never appear in any of the school lists. By contrast, seven poems account for nearly half the occurrences. These are: 'Spleen IV' (37 occurrences); 'L'invitation au voyage' (36); 'Correspondances' (36); 'Parfum exotique' (31); 'L'albatros' (31); 'La vie antérieure '(29) and 'Harmonie du soir' (20). Most of these poems are actually parts of the section *Spleen et Idéal*. Thus we can observe that the school lists are usually made up of texts from the first part of *Les Fleurs du mal*, despite the fact that this section represents only 66 per cent of the poems in the whole collection.

Different explanations for these choices can be suggested. The context in which poetry is studied is probably significant. Different types of technical or material constraints in schools probably account in part for some of the teachers' choices. The longest poems are usually abandoned because they are considered impractical for study in the classroom. We never find, for example, 'Danse macabre', 'Rêve parisien', or 'Une martyre', all of which are around sixty lines in length. 'Benediction' (66 lines) and 'L'irréparable' (50 lines) are found only once on the list. Teachers therefore make their own personal choices while working within the practical constraints of the classroom. This is perhaps not surprising.

On the other hand, we can see that of the seven poems most frequently chosen, three are sonnets, two are only 16 lines long, and only 'L'invitation au voyage' extends beyond one page (in some editions). In the whole corpus of the *Fleurs du mal*, the sonnets represent a total of 41.5 per cent of the selected texts. This number is not very different from the proportion of sonnets in the whole collection. Consequently, studying the sonnet as an emblematic form for poetry seems to be obligatory in the last year of secondary school. Sonnets represent 2.7 of the 6.6 poetry texts that appear on the school list.

It is worth noting that in addition to the list of texts, different literary problems were also frequently mentioned. Analysis of these problems is useful because it reveals no indication whatever of what a sonnet is, as a poetic form. The variety in the short poems of fourteen lines could have been a good approach to studying *Les Fleurs du mal*. However, studies of Baudelaire's poetics which appear in the lists comprise an important number of sonnets. Therefore, it appears that the choice of pieces, in other words the constitution of a specific Baudelairian corpus, is connected with specific teaching constraints and is influenced again by teachers' choice.

The order of the texts on the lists can also be seen as an indicator of the different study lines followed in class. In twenty-nine lists, the order is exactly the same as in Baudelaire's original. The main tendency is to begin with the first poem of the collection, or one of the very first. However, this does not necessarily mean that this order corresponds exactly to the chronological order adopted in class. Nonetheless, this order does reveal that reflection on the structure (construction or progression) of the collection may have been a subject of study in class. At least it shows the teachers' respect for Baudelaire's words: 'le seul éloge que je sollicite pour ce livre est qu'on reconnaisse qu'il n'est pas un pur album et qu'il a un commencement et une fin' (Lettre de Vigny, 1861).

Interpretative connections

Our hypothesis is that the text of *Les Fleurs du mal*, as revealed by the lists, is probably determined by the meaning ordinarily given to it, as far as reading at secondary school is concerned. The choice of representative texts depends on a hypothesis about the construction of the whole work. To try to solve this problem, let us start from the text that appears most frequently in the lists, 'L'invitation au voyage'.

This text appears 83 times in the text groupings, and 37 times among the 69 studies of the complete *Fleurs du mal*. This represents an occurrence of one in five. Then, if we list the pieces which appear together with 'L'invitation au voyage', we can bring to light what we can call (with Charles S. Peirce) the 'Baudelairian interpreters' of this text.

Table 7.4 presents the results of this analysis.

Table 7.4 *Concurrence of different texts with 'L'invitation au voyage'*

Text	Occurrences	Percentage
'L'invitation au voyage'	83	100%
'Parfum exotique'	39	62%
'La vie antérieure'	25	56%
'Le voyage'	24	70%
'Correspondances'	16	26%
'L'albatros'	11	22%
'Spleen IV'	11	15%

The figures in Table 7.4 represent the concurrence of the different texts with 'L'invitation au voyage' in the text groupings. The percentages show the connection between these concurrences and the total number of occurrences of each text in the groupings. For example, 62 per cent of the occurrences of 'Parfum exotique' concur with 'L'invitation au voyage'.

Table 7.5 represents, in decreasing order, the texts which are the most frequent in the text groupings.

Table 7.5 *Texts which are the most frequent in the text groupings*

Text	Occurrences
'L'invitation au voyage'	83
'Spleen IV'	73
'Parfum exotique'	62
'Correspondances'	56
'L'albatros'	50
'La vie antérieure'	44
'A une passante'	40
'L'ennemi'	35
'Le voyage'	34

The same analysis in the corpus of complete works produces the following results.

Table 7.6 *The most frequent texts in the corpus of complete works*

Text	Occurrences
'Spleen IV'	37
'L'invitation au voyage'	36
'Correspondances'	36
'Parfum exotique'	31
'L'albatros'	31
'La vie antérieure'	29
'Harmonie du soir'	20
'Chant d'automne'	16
'A une passante'	13

Table 7.7 *The most frequent concurrences with 'L'invitation au voyage' in the corpus of complete works*

Text	Occurrences
'Spleen IV'	19
'Parfum exotique'	17
'Correspondances'	17
'La vie antérieure'	16
'L'albatros'	16
'Chant d'automne'	13
'Harmonie du soir'	13
'A une passante'	9

If we compare Table 7.4 and Table 7.5, we see that the same texts appear in both tables, but the hierarchy is different. It is interesting to note some of these differences, for example, for 'Spleen IV', 'La vie antérieure' or 'Le voyage'. It means that the groupings which contain 'L'invitation au voyage' have a peculiar configuration. They are based on a series of poems which could not be deduced from a simple statistical analysis of the most frequent texts found in the collection.

On the other hand, a comparison of Tables 7.6 and 7.7 shows the same hierarchy in the two tables. This suggests that in the groupings, the texts chosen by the teachers are dependant. If 'L'invitation au voyage' is chosen, we can predict the series of other texts which will appear in the same grouping. Thus we can assume that the texts which appear together in a text grouping share an interpretative connection. Each text in a grouping is what Charles S. Peirce calls 'an interpreter' of the others. This connection gives a precise basis for the text grouping. However, with respect to the reading of *Les Fleurs du mal* as a complete work, we cannot make this prediction. In this case, texts are chosen only because they constitute a representative group from the whole work.

There are two significant conclusions to be drawn from these results. First, even when the teaching purpose is an extensive reading of the complete work from beginning to end, we see that the real practice at school is to read a kind of digest, which is statistically predictable. Second, when the texts are collected in a so-called consistent grouping based on some theme or literary problem, the frame of such a grouping is predictable, that is, the model of the interpretation itself.

Constituting study themes

We propose now to consider the thematic structure of the text groupings in which 'L'invitation au voyage' appears. As far as the groupings containing 'L'invitation au voyage' are concerned, the titles of 30 of them contain the word 'voyage'. Ten other titles contain a synonym such as *évasion, villeurs, exotisme*. Thus we can conclude that nearly half (40 out of 83) the groupings in question make the noun *voyage*, which is part of the title itself, a prevailing theme.

A second group can be constituted by groupings organized around the theme of 'woman': for example, 'Feminine figures in Baudelaire's and Nerval's works: from sensuality to redemption'; 'The poet and the woman' etc. It seems, in this case, that the chosen theme does not come directly from the poem title, but rather from the phrase ('Mon enfant ma soeur ...') which reveals the addressee of the *invitation*.

The feminine theme, a leading theme like *le voyage*, emphasizes what the text is about, and its immediate purpose.

Thus, 'L'invitation au voyage' appears in groupings whose thematic coherence is based on the obvious terms of the text, without any distinction being made between the enunciative status of discourse reference and the discourse addressee. The specific dimension of the literary text can be forgotten in the name of the thematic identity of the content. The text grouping is constituted in reference to what the text says, not in reference to what it *means* (or signifies).

CONCLUSION

- In comparison with other European countries, for example, Britain, poetry appears to be quite well represented in the corpus of school literature at secondary level in France.
- However, some limitations are involved in the structure of this poetic corpus. For example, there are specific limitations related to the extension of the corpus itself. Poetry at school appears to be drawn predominantly from the Romantic or post-Romantic periods. Indeed, Baudelaire can be now considered as *the* school poet. There are also limitations

concerning the interpretations of the corpus. The analysis of our data shows that there is a school interpretation of Baudelaire, revealed by the structure of the text groupings that have been observed.
- The reading of poetry seems to focus generally on the *denoted* meaning, instead of taking account of the specificity of the literature.

FUTURE DIRECTIONS

Finally, I shall end with a plan for future research. This study is not yet complete. We intend to continue this description with an annual review of the oral literature tests as set by the *baccalauréat*. We are planning an in-depth study of a different *academie* each year. So, in time, we shall be able to offer a comprehensive analysis of the trends within and across the *academies*. This annual monitoring will make it possible to note trends and changes that occur in the teaching of poetry and literature within the French secondary school system.

Chapter 8

The Teaching of Poetry in the Netherlands since 1968

Willem de Moor

INTRODUCTION

Since 1968, when the so-called Mammouth Law was introduced, the school system in the Netherlands has changed from a selective system (with gymnasium, lyceum and *hogere burger* schools) to a more open system. The change was reflected immediately in the character of the school population, which was also at that time under the wider influences of the worldwide growth of counter- and youth culture. Now, once again, the Dutch school system is facing enormous changes. From September 1993, Dutch basic education provision (*basisvorming*) will become more like the British comprehensive school system where students of all levels are taught together until their sixteenth birthday.

A direct consequence of the introduction of that Mammouth Law for literary education was that fewer children came on to secondary school with ideas about arts and literature. The new system has become very complicated. Few children now enjoy a school career in only two schools, one primary and one secondary. Instead, four or five schools are becoming increasingly the norm. The consequences for literary education, especially reading poetry, have been unfortunate. There is another big change which is already embarrassing teachers in secondary schools. In the proposed *basisvorming* curriculum there is no space for reading poetry, only for reading fiction.

The *goals* have changed. In 1968 appreciation of literary education as a means of increasing our knowledge of our cultural heritage still predominated. Quite clearly, this was impossible for the new school population. So, as in the United States, England, Germany and the Scandinavian countries, we in the Netherlands have adapted our own philosophy of education. In addition, the effects of our civil and social revolution (remember 1966, the marriage of Beatrix and Claus, riots everywhere, especially in Amsterdam, the effects of flower power and student revolts in 1968, followed by the Marxist movement which remained very strong until 1980) influenced the attitude of pupils as well as younger and middle-aged teachers. They wanted literature just for pleasure or for insights into social behaviour. Now, however, Dutch teachers are more and more convinced that we can no longer accept the *laisser faire/laissez aller* policy of the 1970s and 1980s. The new aim is called 'literary competence' and is especially directed at the reading of literature.

This 'literary competence' is quite different from the discussions we had during the Durham Poetry Symposium. The term is restricted to mean the ability to read (and find) literature (fiction, essay, drama and poetry).

THE BOOKS

The books used in the classroom reflect these changes in many ways. In Nijmegen we examined several books from the early 1970s and 1980s with regard to content, the appearance of old and famous authors (like Vondel and Hooft), the position of poetry and prose and so on.

In 1988 we started our Dutch Anthology Project. The project examines anthologies in general but specifically those used for school purposes. We have tried to describe how they are built up, which authors and texts have been collected in which books, the period they cover, and the anthologist(s). We have tried to identify the criteria by which we may distinguish one anthology from another one. We have already discovered the ways in which some anthologists confirm the existing canon of literary works through their choices and we have seen that other anthologists propose to reconstruct a new canon by their choices. However, the project has stopped temporarily, although it remains very interesting and exciting. We hope to find the means to hand over this task to new young researchers soon. However, at the moment the situation in the Netherlands and England is similar. It is quite clear that teachers as well as pupils are much more interested in reading fiction (particularly short stories) than they are in reading poetry.

PROCEDURES

Procedures and ways of teaching have changed most of all. There have been a number of influences on teaching. Didactics of literature and poetry, the reader-response critics in the United States and Scandinavia, and (on the other hand) the more social Malte Dahrendorf c.s. in the BRD have all made it possible to discern workable procedures and methodologies. Pupil-centred methods now exist next to text-centred methods. Steven Ten Brinke, in his book *The Complete Mother-tongue Curriculum* (1976), writes about 'text-studying' and 'text-experiencing' procedures. In this chapter I want to elaborate on the distinctions he makes. My own opinion is that reflectivity is the keyword for poetry-reading in the curriculum. We try to teach the students the ability to reflect constantly on their progress in the learning process. 'Readers' logs', the so-called 'reading files', the 'reader's autobiography' and 'learner reports' are the instruments for this 'reflectivity'.

The term 'reflectivity' has to be interpreted as the ability of people to develop constant reflection on their behaviour, their progress in the learning process and their personal development. It was first mentioned in 1985 in a publication by Harm Damsma. I have thought about this concept for literary education. My main concern is with the concept of object and subject experience (as explained by Robert Witkin in his book *The Intelligence of Feeling*) and with Alan C. Purves's notion of the 'expressed response'. But 'reflectivity' is for me the final keyword in a chain of keywords. This is an idea which I presented in a number of works during the 1980s and which I am still concerned with now.

THE 'MELOPEE' METHOD OF RESPONDING TO POETRY: AN INTRODUCTION

Very often researchers and innovators in our field present their ideas as the one and only solution to all problems. But when we think of the growing opposition among teachers, caused by disappointing years of trying out somebody else's ideas, we must agree that the best way for a teacher to survive is versatility and the best way for the innovator to be accepted is modesty.

Doing things differently from day to day and from hour to hour seems to be a good starting point. Each class is different and experiences changes in mood and character several times during a semester, or a week, or even a day. When you have already worked with small groups twice in one day it can be rather boring and discouraging for you, as the teacher, to do it a third time. When you are losing interest you are losing persuasiveness. So for a change start a classroom discussion or just give a lecture.

Recognizing this problem as an important obstacle in trying to achieve high quality teaching, I have developed a range of options for a literature teacher. They are, of course, developed for teachers in the Netherlands but a comparison between literary education practice in my country and that of the United States, which I had a chance to observe during my three months stay in 1987 as a Fulbright Professor, showed me that in classroom practice exactly the same problems turn up. It is important that we are aware of the decisions and choices we can make as teachers, although I believe many of us are not.

That is why I would like to present you first with a simple model as a reminder of our possibilities. Most of the options will be very familiar to you. I will discuss only two, those between 'text studying' approaches and 'text experiencing' procedures, and between 'author's text' and 'reader's text', in some detail in order to show the consequences of our decisions. I am really proud to be able to do this by means of a poem which used to be rather popular in the Netherlands and Flanders. 'Melopee' by Paul van Ostaijen is a lovely example of our almost neglected poetry.

The last few years should have taught us not to condemn certain methods too quickly. We think some methods are more traditional than others. Sometimes it happens that a method which is considered so old-fashioned today that it will probably be forgotten by tomorrow suddenly becomes very popular again and is seen as an example of progress. No matter how careful we are about accepting or condemning certain methods, it remains important to keep an eye on what exactly we are doing. It seems important for literary education that, on the basis of the knowledge of the various possibilities, we try more and more to come to a deliberate choice of lesson content and teaching procedures.

What I offer here are a number of distinctions into which the teaching procedure can be divided. It is obvious that the list of distinctions can be extended and that the teacher does not always have to make a choice between two elements of a distinction but can aim at a synthesis of the two. I will try to show that sometimes this will be possible, sometimes not. Finally, though I call the first part of the distinction 'more or less traditional' and the second part 'more or less alternative', this does not mean that I am in favour of the distinction in all cases. For me, the main object was to oppose these matters directly for once, and so make it possible for us as teachers to make a choice.

OPTIONS FOR A LITERATURE TEACHER

I shall discuss each of the following options in turn. First there are four distinctions concerning the kind of *reading* we practise:

1. between the *text studying approach* and the *text experiencing strategy*, the ultimate object of which is a significant integration of both components
2. between *intensive* and *extensive* reading. Here too the point is to come to an appropriate interweaving of methods
3. between an *academic* way of reading, such as we do in school, and the *normal* way of reading that we do at home. One should always keep this difference in mind
4. between working towards a *literal understanding* of the text and a *broad understanding* of the text.

A second range of distinctions is that of the *setting*:

- between a literary education that starts with the 15- and 16-year-old student and one that is written out in a *longitudinal curriculum*, from mother's lap or father's knee, so to speak, to the bosom of Alma Mater!
- between *class level* teaching and teaching focused on the *individual*
- between literary education that *focuses on the subject material* and literary education that *focuses on the student*. One could think of a synthesis into a *triadic* literary education, in which teacher, text and pupil are on the same level of importance.

The following five points are interesting for the process of literary education itself. They are also concerned with distinctions:

1. between the *belles lettres* and the *literary history* as subject matter and a *variety of texts*: translated works, the trivial alongside great literary works, reference next to fiction and other literary works
2. between a *chronological* order of literature and a quite different one, for instance a *thematic* arrangement
3. between *author's text* and *reader's text* (I will explain that point later, it is the core of this chapter)
4. between *cognitive* and *confluent* aims and aspects (both affective and cognitive at the same time)
5. between *one-sidedness* in teaching procedures (reading, analyzing and writing only) and *versatility* (discussions, dramatization, drawing etc.).

My last range of distinctions is concerned with the teacher's choices in *testing*:

- between mainly *convergent* questions and assignments and *divergent* and *evaluative* assignments
- between *long-term evaluation* in the form of exams and *short-term evaluation* in the form of reading reports, dicussions, creative assignments and the like
- between a decisive role for the *internal examination* and a decisive role for the so-called *reading file* or *reader's log*.

Text studying and text experiencing approach

After presenting you with this list of distinctions, I would like to concentrate firstly on this one: the distinction between the text studying and text experiencing approach.

All sources agree that up to the present time, literary education has been to a large extent determined by development in literary theory. From the beginning of the 1970s the methodology of literary education has been developing and trying to link up a number of ideas about teaching the reading of literature. Maybe it would be advisable, and more in accordance with what you as a teacher are going to try out, not to be biased about the prevailing view in literary theory. Literary education ought to discover which elements from the successive areas of special attention in the theory of literature, namely the author, the text and the reader, can be used in teaching literature.

Research reveals that in many cases the motivation of the students is hampered by the fact that the texts have to be analyzed, carved up into ready chunks. This is what I call *the approach by way of textual analysis*. The source of this approach is clear: the subject-centred education which results in attention being paid to the reading list and its long-term (summative) evaluation; the tendency to treat literature in a chronological order; the tendency to impart literal understanding of a text and the nature of the questions connected with it.

It would be incorrect to conclude immediately that text studying approaches fail by definition and that therefore it is time to turn to other strategies. The literary text is plainly an extremely important part of the subject matter, and attention to the text and questions about it are essential for a sound teaching of literature. There are plenty of teachers who show us that the text studying approach, presented in an enthusiastic way, can positively bring about effective teaching. The notion of text studying covers all the activities of the reader that fall within the design:

READER >> TEXT

Activities which, in other words, are directed towards understanding a text by way of analysis. The text studying approach in the classroom includes all forms of teaching literature in which the teacher tries to convey to the student an understanding of the literary text without paying explicit attention to the effect the text exerts on the student.

The notion of *text experience*, on the other hand, covers the spontaneous as well as the repeated, further affecting experience of the text by the student according to the pattern

TEXT >> READER

By text experiencing strategies are meant all forms of teaching literature in which the teacher pays explicit attention to the effect of the text on the student and aims at the realization of a process that makes the student aware of the affective and cognitive values that the text has or does not have from the student's point of view.

Author's text – reader's text

Depending on what you are trying to achieve, you can either opt for the text studying approach and look for the author's text, or you can opt for the text experiencing strategy and try to discover the reader's text. A third possibility is, of course, a combination of the two.

I would like to demonstrate this by way of the poem 'Melopee', written in 1925 by the Flemish poet Paul van Ostaijen. The reason I have chosen this poem to illustrate both distinctions is because of the nature of the text experiencing strategy presented here, namely, making a drawing after reading a text. 'Melopee' is a very expressive poem; the poet has been very clear about its meaning, and so it is possible to reconstruct the author's text (the author's poem). Apart from that, it contains poetic elements which make a whole range of interpretations possible. This makes a comparison between various reader's texts very interesting, not only for the reception-aesthetician or literary didactician but also for teachers and pupils.

In 1959 Gunnar Hansson put forward his distinction between what he termed *the author's text and the reader's text*. The author's text can be defined as 'the reconstruction of a process of creation (starting points, origin of motives, meanings, feelings and thoughts) of the contents of the lines of the poem, including the personal meanings and motives behind it'. Gunnar Hansson added: 'The writer has made this known in, for example, personal commentary, letters, interviews etc.'

The author's text, then, gives the interpretation that includes the complete intentions of the author, or at least comes as close to it as possible. In my view, the reconstruction is completed when all the professional interpretations of a particular text are set alongside utterances from the author.

At least as crucial for education is the acknowledgement of the importance of reader's texts. These arise from the personal frame of reference of each individual reader, for whom reading words, sentences, the description of objects or events etc., has its own personal associations. In Mukarovsky's terminology one can say that the *artefact* (the actual book, the paper with the letters) remains constant but the *aesthetic object* (what the reader sees in what he (or she) reads, what he makes of it) changes continually. For the reader is dependent on the literary conventions of the time and the environment and there is always a personal history colouring this perception.

Iser's view (1970) is similar to this. A literary or other text never offers a world that is exactly the same as the reader's. Because of the difference between the text that covers the world of the author and the text that grows within the reader (as an aesthetic object), there arises what Iser calls *Unbestimmtheit*. This vagueness (or indefiniteness) works as an important link between the text and the reader. It activates the imagination of the reader. This is what Iser calls *external working*. But there is also something like *internal working* which arises from the presence of the so-called *Leerstellen*, or open spots. In every literary text the reader has to complete certain elements for himself. A good novelist leaves much to the imagination, a bad one explains everything. The open spots appear to be essential for the aesthetic response of the reader; they, too, activate the reader. Trivial literature can be boring because it does not contain open spots.

THE TEXT

Now let us have a look at the poem, 'Melopee' by Paul van Ostaijen.

> Under the moon slides the long river
> Across the long river slides the tired moon
> Under the moon on the long river the canoe slides towards the sea

Past the high reed
past the low meadow
the canoe slides towards the sea
the canoe with the sliding moon slides towards the sea
Thus they are companions towards the sea the canoe the moon and the man
Why do the moon and the man slide meekly together towards the sea

The author's text

Now I would like to tell you something about the place of the argument in van Ostaijen's *œuvre* and in particular emphasize the information that can tell us something about the author's intention.

'Melopee' is one of a group of poems that appeals to children because of the fun they have in playing around with language, because of its descriptive character and appeal to the imagination. The poem was written in 1925. The author's intention we are looking for becomes clear when we consider van Ostaijen's views on poetry in 1925 and 1926. The sources for this information are a lecture called: 'Specimen of parallels between modern plastic arts and modern literature' given by the author on 3 September 1925 in Breda. In *Self Defence*, a series of very interesting notes on his own poetry, he says that all the poems written between 1921 and 1926 contain no more than the thematic development of a preconceived sentence, as for example in 'Melopee': 'Under the moon slides the long river'. 'Here I speak of a form that, for me, expresses my aspirations most profoundly.'

Another quotation from van Ostaijen's *Self Defence* is:

> Poetry = wordart. Poetry is not: thought, mind, beautiful sentences, is neither doctoral nor dada. It simply is play with words anchored down in the metaphysical.

With van Ostaijen, metaphysical does not refer so much to the supernatural as to the subconscious. With this we are getting close to the heart of the matter, the reason why, in the Netherlands especially, the poets from the 1950s saw van Ostaijen as a forerunner. The art of the *écrire automatique* is as much part of their programme as it was of the Flemish expressionist who lived twenty years earlier.

As a teacher I visualize the poem on the basis of the reading experiences offered by professional readers, insofar as I am not able to check all the utterances made by the poet himself. Thus two critics (Uyttersprot and Kazemier) have pointed out that van Ostaijen sees a distinction between his *lyrisme-à-thème* or *poèsie-à-thème* and the poetry that is about something else, which is called the *poèsie-à-sujet*. His poem grows because one word evokes another. The same two critics point out four items that have influenced the creation of 'Melopee':

- The general course of the poem is determined by the intention to write a 'melopee', described in Dutch dictionaries as 'a monotonous singing' or 'a piece of music with an undefined melody'. I refer to the singing of the muezzin in the minaret to announce the afternoon with its obligatory prayer: an undefined melody passing away into thin air.
- The first sentence must be the most positive (= assertive).
- The following sentences will be more and more indefinable. Van Ostaijen tries to achieve this by lengthening the first sentence with a new subject and an additional modification of circumstances.
- A caesura will probably be necessary to give the next lines a notion of distance.

There is yet another variant of van Ostaijen's *lyrisme à thème* if we call 'Melopee' an example of 'organic expressionism'. It does not mean to be a human avowal, a display of personal joy, grief or passion; its origin is purely aesthetic and it means only to evoke an aesthetic emotion.

One of the critics mentioned previously, also says that van Ostaijen's poem is related to Edgar Allen Poe's 'The Raven'. Briefly, both poets have similar aims:

- to achieve a purely aesthetic working of the lyrical poem
- the poem must be very short otherwise it would deteriorate, and that is why Van Ostaijen repeatedly says he will limit himself to 12 or 13 verse lines; the rest should be cut off
- the perfect poem is a product not only of pure inspiration but also of choosing sounds, meanings, rhythm etc.

I would like to quote a last piece of information given by the author himself, who says: 'I try to let the idea speak only through the rhythm ... for example the endless weariness is not explicitly mentioned in Melopee, you can only hear the *sound* of it'.

Apparently van Ostaijen's intention was to evoke an endless weariness, by starting from one sentence, letting a more or less absolute certainty slip into vagueness and by using more lengthy sentences. The reader should have an aesthetic experience or emotion because of this. If you want to evaluate the author's poem you can check for yourself whether or not this intention has been achieved!

Readers' texts

Once the poet has completed and published his text, it is then the reader's turn, both the professional and the everyday reader. They reproduce, quoting Hansson (1959), Holland (1975) and Iser (1974), the reader's text. To be more precise, they produce *their* reader's text. We assume, then, that there are as many reader's texts as there are readers looking at the poem. With this marginal note, one reader can have different reader's texts every time the poem is read anew.

Within the school and the classroom, I would like to make a distinction between teacher's text and student's text. Because the teacher already knows the text, has read critics' opinions about it and reflected on it, he or she can come up with several interpretations representing many products of reader's perceptions. Because of the teacher's position in class, this knowledge will very often influence the reception of the text by the students. We should be more aware of this. Very often the students are given a whole range of notes by the teacher, even before they have had a chance to read the text for themselves. Undoubtedly this prevents an open-minded reception of a new text.

The teacher's text

Let us assume that I, as a teacher, know all the information that critics have written on 'Melopee'. I could pass this knowledge on to my students; tell them that they do not necessarily have to look for a deeper meaning, or that the question in the last line does not require an answer. As an excuse for all this, I could say that a 'melopee' is just a range of sounds and words that pass away into thin air and that nobody has shown better what a 'melopee' is than van Ostaijen whose poem is summarized by critics as: 'monotonous, melodious, with female rhyme, heaving and without explosion'.

I am not going to bore my pupils with remarks about the soft gliding initial *sl-* , even if it is a quite interesting phenomenon in itself and is found occurring more frequently in van Ostaijen's work; or with the remark that 'tired' in line 2 means 'a rhythmic lift and a lingering'. I would establish that the poet certainly is deviating from his initial intention not to express the endless weariness. I would be more careful as far as 'the delicate lift that brings languor' suggested in lines 1, 2 and 3 is concerned. I am very much inclined to leave the critics' comments where they are and complete my personal didactical analysis of the poem by pointing out certain facts that seem to be important for me as a teacher. This may be knowledge that can be useful in a conversation about the poem. For example, the endlessness, the endless weariness that van Ostaijen has written about, I find in 'the long river', a phrase recurring in three different places in the first three sentences. In particular, it is the verb 'slide' (recurring seven times in lines 1, 2, 3, 6, 7 (twice) and 9) that calls to mind the endless continuation. This is also the case with the prepositions of place at the beginning of lines 1, 2, 3 and 4/5: they get lengthier every time.

The student's text(s)

'What dream does "Melopee" arouse in you, reader?', a critic asks at the end of his essay. I in my turn asked my students this question. To collect the answers I could have used familiar conversation techniques, possibly combining them with creative writing assignments (for example, using Bleich's method of retelling by exploring the affective and associative response). For these I could have used the atmosphere of the poem as a starting point for their own descriptions of a series of comparable images. Because 'Melopee' is so very visual I approached it differently: drawing pictures in combination with a classroom discussion.

Objects and procedure

The objects I pursued were:

- to challenge the students to look very carefully
- to get the students to exchange views about their perception and interpretation of the poem
- to make the students aware of the possibilities of understanding the poem and adapting it by drawing a picture of it
- to promote working together.

The procedure of the lesson was as follows:

- The poem was presented anonymously to a total of 103 students. They were split up into 28 groups of three or four students. They were asked, firstly, to read the poem for themselves for five minutes and write a very short summary, then to talk about the poem together in the small groups of three or four. Previous knowledge of van Ostaijen's *œuvre* hardly played any part. Then I asked them to picture the poem as concretely or abstractly as they wanted.
- After about half an hour of reading, writing and talking about the poem the groups needed a further 15 minutes to make the final drawing. I am presuming that secondary school pupils do not need longer because they will probably not go into the poem deeply. Also

in every class there may be one or two pupils who will start drawing spontaneously and almost immediately.
- The drawings were made using thick pencils on big sheets of paper that were displayed in the classroom when completed. Sometimes explanations were given, sometimes a discussion followed. Through these conversations the groups showed the whole class what views they held. This can expand the student's own view. Showing the different pieces of work is important for the satisfaction of the students. The results not only showed some very ingenious points of view but also some very nice pictures. Explicit attention was paid to every single piece of work.

However, the most important result of this procedure is due to the first phase. This became clear to me because the appreciation the students showed for the first phase was greater than for what followed. I have no reason to presume this would be different in secondary school but it would be useful to verify it. Tape-recordings made of the different group discussions made clear the two tasks each group had to fulfil:

- to come to an agreement about the interpretation of the poem, and
- find a way to picture this interpretation that was acceptable to each member of the group.

As a teacher I often mentioned that the picture did not have to be at all beautiful, as long as it indicated what the group meant. However, if they wanted to make the most of it they should choose the best artist for the task. They usually produced a group drawing but in two cases individual members of the group made their own picture.

Results: A selection of student's texts

If one looks at the protocols of the group discussions (tape-recordings were made but cannot be reproduced here), it appears that the students came up with a great number of points even though they stuck closely to the subject. Comparing the student's text with the teacher's or author's text you can see that especially the elements of slackening down and the endless weariness – pictured here as helplessness – are found spontaneously; the arguments all arise from the text itself.

It is remarkable that the decisions about what picture to draw were made under pressure of time but this did not seem to be detrimental. The results corresponded with the way of thinking that preceded the drawing of the picture. That this was true for the average drawing became clear from evaluation discussions held after different sessions. In all cases the spokesman/woman managed to match the result with the preceding conversation, sometimes making excuses for the quality of the expression.

Now let us turn our attention to the drawings produced. The first drawing (Figure 8.1) belongs to the relatively small category, three out of 28 drawings, in which the picture of the sliding canoe, the man and the moon and the long river is relinquished. Instead, a leaking tap expresses repetition and endlessness, while the picture of a falling man in a vast space (Figure 8.2) reminds us of man's insignificance and the cosmic life experience which one group tasted in the poem.

The rest of the 28 drawings can be divided into six different categories:

Figure 8.1

Figure 8.2

Figure 8.3

Figure 8.4

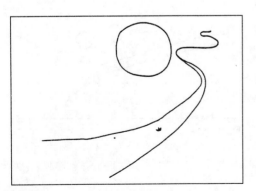

Figure 8.5

Figure 8.6

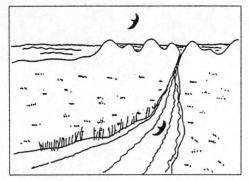

Figure 8.7

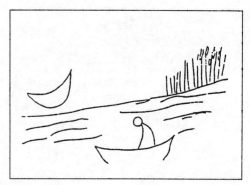

Figure 8.8

Figure 8.9

Figure 8.10

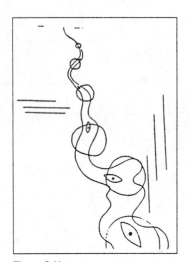

Figure 8.11

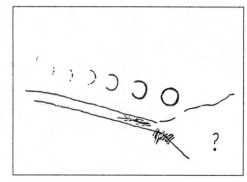

Figure 8.12

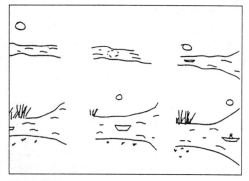

Figure 8.13

Figure 8.14

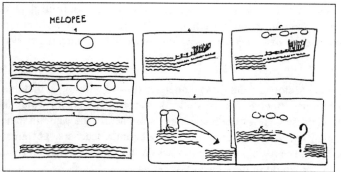

Figure 8.15

- First, the playful, anecdotal reactions. A little man, happily on his way to the sea, the moon like a balloon in one's hand, is merrily singing melopee (this was represented in two drawings).
- Second, linking up with these ideas, six reactions were presented where the man alone in the canoe was the central point. This idea plays a part in all the other reactions but in the second category we constantly see the man on his way to the horizon (Figure 8.3), or from behind (Figure 8.4) or sideways with the moon very large near him or with the crescent moon like a star of Bethlehem in front of him seen from above, or very far away, small and insignificant under the colossal moon (Figure 8.5). Everything refers to being insignificant and alone in nature.
- Remarkable features are the redoubling (in six of the pictures) and the repetition (in five of them). The redoubling is expressed by the resemblance between the moon on the one hand and the man and the canoe on the other hand (Figure 8.6). Outlines are consciously made identical (Figure 8.7), and twice the crescent moon is placed in a very unusual position, lying down, just to resemble a little boat (Figure 8.8). Reflection especially gives the interpretation of a contemplative and introvert character. Obviously these groups were most struck by the strong bond between moon and man that 'Melopee' evokes.

- The many repetitions show, as do the given explanations, that the students were struck with the repetitions in the text, the long river, sliding, the moon, the canoe sliding to the sea. This also becomes clear from the objects used in the repetitions: the moon, the canoe, the river. Four out of five reactions show the moon as well as the canoe with the man (Figure 8.9), one on the increase (Figure 8.10), one from bird's point of view (Figure 8.11), and one shows only the repetition of the moon on the increase (Figure 8.12). These drawings not only give voice to the repetition but also to the aspect of time: the long duration or endlessness of the journey. These five reactions, particularly, show a great similarity to what was expressed in the author's text and the teacher's text.
- The last group of five reactions was rather diverse in their expression. In all cases, students chose a formal-analytic approach. Sometimes they combined a realistic representation with a surrealistic or formal element. Twice every single line of the poem was used to make a comic strip (Figure 8.13). Rather special is the picture in which the canoe and the moon come together in the curve of the question mark of which the river is the stem (Figure 8.14). In van Ostaijen's view, this must be the most adequate reaction to his poem. If he is not looking for a deeper meaning, should we?
- This last case makes clear what the students experienced. This is not quite so clear from the comic strips but that does not mean that those group discussions were not fruitful. One group stressed the question at the end by not visualizing it (Figure 8.13). Another group pictured the poem line by line in very clear drawings combined with referring arrows, stressing the repetitions (Figure 8.15).

Comparing the author's text of 'Melopee' with these reader's texts you will notice that this classroom collaboration can be very effective for the students' scope of the poem, which is not poor or simple but in fact very rich. All of the readers' texts are nearly the same in their meaning as the author's original text. My students, who are all future teachers, got great satisfaction out of this method. Afterwards almost everybody said they were going to try out the described discussion–drawing method in their own classrooms.

In most cases I prefer using only one of the two procedures at a time, although it is possible to combine them. Only then, after the students have constructed texts of their own, do they appear to be curious to know about the author's text.

REFERENCES

Damsma, Harm (1985) *Taalbeschouwing als reflectiviteit* (The Study of Language as an Incentive to Reflectivity). Enschede: SLO.
Hansson, Gunnar (1959) *Dikten och Läsaren*. Uppsala: Bonniers.
Hansson, Gunnar (1973) Some types of research on response to literature. *Research in the Teaching of English*, **7** (2).
Holland, Norman (1975) *5 Readers Reading*. London: Yale University Press.
Iser, Wolfgang (1970) *Die Appelstruktur der Texte*. Konstanz: Universitätsverlag.
van Ostaijen, Paul (1928) *Gedichten*. Antwerpen: De Sikkel.

Chapter 9

Thinking Through Form:
Preparing to Teach Poetry in School

Colin Walter

> *For there are memories that have no name: you don't even know what to ask for.*
> Ciaran Carson

BEGINNING WITH A CLAIM FOR POETRY

If the arts are indeed 'the most scrupulous exploration we can make of our personalities and their relationships' (Hoggart, 1992), teachers deserve support in avoiding a piecemeal or merely occasional treatment in school curricula. The teaching of poetry is neither more nor less desirable than the teaching of the other arts, nor are the ways of setting about it entirely unrelated to, for instance, the teaching of painting or music. Yet the nature of each defines the task, and language is the nature of poetry.

While the teaching of the child's first language is universally endorsed and pursued, discussed, complained about and studied, the teaching of poetry is often attended by confusions and doubts which too often make it the subject of uncomfortable special pleading. At the same time it is insisted that poetry teaching is essential within the teaching of the first language in school; that the processes of becoming literate are indivisible from those which support a response to poetry – and that this is so because of the role of poetry within language and languages. The National Curriculum for English insists on all of this, but it will be to little effect unless we use an adequate pedagogy.

We need to refer to a more specific and detailed description of how poetry and languages are related, of the kind which Brodsky (1991) implies when he says:

> poetry is not a form of entertainment and in a certain sense not even a form of art but our anthropological, genetic goal, our evolutionary linguistic beacon. We seem to sense that as children when we absorb and remember verses in order to master the language. As adults we abandon the pursuit, convinced that we know enough about it. But what we've mastered is an idiom, good enough to outfox an enemy, sell a product, get laid, or earn promotion, but not enough to cure anguish or cause joy.

The conclusion to which Brodsky is moving here is that without poetry we are *sub-lingual*. Here is a claim for poetry that it represents a peculiar knowledge about language, and offers a utility which, while being greatly extended by literacy, has its origins elsewhere. It is a utility which is vulnerable, now as ever, to a narrow view of literacy and its purposes. For, now as ever, we may be sure that if school curricula only offer young people the means to get by, they never will – anguish not being as easily banished as joy!

BEGINNING TO SEEK A PEDAGOGY FOR POETRY

> *I'd mind if there was no poetry, it's short and doesn't go on and on.*
> Linda, aged 8

... In the primary school

It is what happens to their perceptions and expectations of poetry in the first half of the time they spend at school which enables children to recognize that poetry is not an abstruse intellectual puzzle, nor just another school requirement. These years offer a special opportunity for them to inhabit the knowledge that poetry is a pleasurable use of language offering distinctive ways of thinking. An opportunity to recognize, in use, the distinction between poetry and any particular example of a poem, upon which an ability to 'study' poems during their secondary school years depends.

... In teacher education

Many commentators on the teaching of poetry in school express unease about its effectiveness – and it is very common, still, for teachers to do so. Although this should not be allowed to blind us to the existence of the inspired practice which occurs, the results of misconceptions about the ways and means of poetry teaching have to be addressed.

One of these results is that when young people join teacher education courses, to begin their professional preparation for primary school work, they bring with them the results of the teaching they received at school. This is so whether they join four-year Bachelor of Education programmes straight from school, or join one-year postgraduate teacher education courses.

So, while initial teacher education may be expected, justifiably, to achieve improved professional practice, it faces a number of special challenges. Often it has to begin immediately to develop the young teacher as a mature and willing reader (reading I take to be proof of an individual commitment). At the same time it has to provide them with the means of building a coherent methodology for teaching poetry successfully to young children. It must have strategies which are capable of accommodating widely varying levels of motivation towards, and experience of, valuing poetry. Some students will scarcely have met poetry recently at all, some will have received devoted and wise teaching within English Studies, some will have reacted against an analytical or closely textual approach to teaching, some will have grown used to viewing poetry as just another object for academic study, some will have been introduced to the value of poetry by teachers in quite other disciplines than Literature Studies, and some will have discovered it for themselves, or as a result of the influence of friends or relations.

Brodsky's claim for poetry that it is lingual may, I suggest, inform our search for adequate pedagogies for teaching primary school children, and teacher education alike; and I should like to explore why.

THE BEGINNINGS OF POETRY FOR CHILDREN AND TEACHERS

Poetry happens in the minimum of space and the minimum of time, and that in itself makes it modern and gives it a future.

Miroslav Holub

Many writers, across intellectual disciplines, refer to languages possessing 'a poetic function', of which poetry is one result. However incomplete any description of this poetic function may be, it offers a ready conceptualization within a description of language, of the value and accessibility of poetry to all speakers.

Jakobson's (1960) description of the poetic function as a formal property of language suggests ways that we can summarize some of the origins of children's predilection for poetry, and conceive of a classroom pedagogy which builds upon children's previous language learning. To this end we may adopt both phylogenetic and ontogenetic approaches to the origins of poetry within language.

A phylogenetic focus notes the ubiquity of poetry within human communities. This has led some commentators to suggest that poetry and language have common origins (Langer, 1942). It acknowledges the centrality of proto-poetic experience and oral poetry within the lives of pre-literate communities, as sources of memory and explanation, for instance within ritual (Geertz, 1983). Further, it directs our interest in defining the changing role of poetry within literate communities. It may, I suggest, offer a useful perspective from which to consider the growth of children's commitment to poetry in school – within the company of other children.

An ontogenetic focus notes the history of proto-poetic experience with language, with chant, song, and rhyme, in play, within children's early lives, of which their experience of poetry teaching at school is a development. It notes, too, how children's playground lives are a continuation of much that they did previously. This can be evident on a number of occasions, for example, during their very earliest learning of speech when progress towards independent thought and identity is marked by 'enacting' metaphor (Vygotsky, 1978a); and during the process by which parents, and others at home, induct children into the ways of their culture by means of songs and action in play; and, similarly, during the incipient co-operation and social interaction with the limited number of other children with whom they come into contact.

Upon reaching school, the society of other children becomes a main feature of childhood, most immediately in the playground. There indeed, along the spectrum of joy and anguish, children exist in a relationship as significant to each other as form is to language. There, too, within an oral culture of play in language, we find the reproduction of a number of the phylogenetic features of the poetic function of language.

In setting out upon the teaching of poetry we can best proceed, I want to suggest, by seeking to transfer specific features of the playground world of children into the literate world of the classroom. There, as children gain the company of others, they may as naturally begin to achieve the possibilities offered by an interaction with poems as texts.

Teaching poetry from the beginning: private and public exchange

*A good poem
should smell of tea*

Olav Hauge

The principle I should like to refer to here is as relevant to teaching young teachers as young children, I believe. For the sake of brevity I shall refer, mostly, to teaching young children.

Beginning to teach young children to be willing readers and makers of poems entails the use of teaching strategies which will gradually unlock resources in a reading culture of which children are becoming members. Their enjoyment of poems interacts with a recognition of the enjoyment of other readers, writers, tellers and listeners, within a community of childhood making sense of shared experience – both of poems and what the poems refer to.

Watching this happen over a number of years has demonstrated, to me, that distinction which Vygotsky draws between learning and development, as he describes learning as creating a 'zone of proximal development'. This is learning which 'awakens a variety of internal development processes that are able to operate only when the child is interacting with people in his environment and in co-operation with his peers' (Vygotsky, 1978b: 90).

Thus our pedagogy must sow in order to reap later. Then, as a result of children living, often for quite a short time, within a culture of response and composition, they may write something which even up to the point of its composition seemed beyond their ability. An example of similar development is described by Slobin and Welsh (1971), in the study of the 2-year-old child, Echo, learning to speak the syntax of English. You will remember how, sitting at breakfast surrounded by everything familial and breakfasty, she was able to volunteer syntactic constructions in speech which half an hour afterwards, away from the table, she was not able to repeat accurately.

The classroom strategies we need should establish specific kinds of interactions between learning and development, and between contexts and intentions in learners, over a period of time. These interactions originate, I suggest, in the phylogenetic and ontogenetic predisposition to poetry already noted. We seek thereby to build in children a commitment to reading which includes the private reading of poems, derived from a tacit understanding that the pleasures and meanings issue from what happens *as* they read. It happens from children engaging in one kind of concentration rather than another (Rosenblatt, 1978).

In these ways children are able to begin as readers and writers, and they do so as they become interactive and progressively interdependent. A teacher may begin in the following way with a class of 8- and 9-year-olds (Year 4/Year 5).

For example, each child is given three carefully selected author collections of appropriate poems for children, for use at school and at home. This is the first of a number of strategies to regularize children's private and public reading aloud, their listening and their writing, and their reflection upon the results of all of these. Immediately the teacher might suggest that everyone should collect together poems that they particularly like by writing them out in a special book. Then, at weekly meetings, children might read aloud previously selected poems from these growing personal anthologies. For these meetings, the class is best divided into two parts. They do not, of course, even have to meet on the same day each week. It is only important that the meetings occur regularly and are timetabled. Soon children will want to try writing poems of their own. Then, at the author's discretion, these too may also be included in the anthologies. Then, if the children choose to, they may read them aloud at the weekly meetings.

These few strategies will establish patterns of exchange and interaction between children and poems, both outside and inside the classroom, and the participation of other members of the social worlds to which the children belong. All of this may be further promoted by the use of a poetry table in the classroom.

The poetry table

Its beginnings are simple, though at best they are expertly presented to the class as a surprise one morning, in the form of twelve or so fresh and well-selected author-collections on an attractively labelled, arranged and positioned table. Behind, on the wall, the teacher may have put, typed out, some poems which children have previously enjoyed in the weekly meetings.

My interest in this strategy lies in its contribution to the culture of exchange which has begun to grow. For instance, children may not only begin to use the table at set times as a source of private reading, but also informally in many previously unspecified ways. They will initiate many and various patterns of solitary reading, shared reading with close friends, and the habitual sharing of discoveries with whoever is nearby. Should the teacher suggest that they may choose to bring books of poems from home to leave on the table for a short time during the day, this would only complement the original suggestion by the teacher that children should use school books at home, and vice versa. Moreover it would be a suggestion aimed at endorsing what the teacher knows will have been going on outside the classroom as a result of earlier activity.

The request for children to collect poems in a context of enjoyment, and further select from these to read to other children, will ensure that they start to read poems outside the classroom. Children should be encouraged to compose outside the classroom too. All of this activity should be initiated by the children themselves. Within this context there is every reason for the teacher to be confident that books will begin to appear from home.

We have already reminded ourselves of why we may anticipate that many members of the wider community value poetry, and the teacher's suggestion therefore simply endorses those reasons. Also, children's enthusiasm, directly expressed at home, can be a powerful influence on any parent! So, in respect of books, there will be few children who are not able to bring collections of nursery rhymes saved from earlier days. For these to appear early on the poetry table supports all the assumptions about poetry that we are trying to encourage at this early stage. Then, to 'assume' the presence of poetry books at home is often to create it. We can be sure that the children will already be sharing poems they have found with parents and others at home. The responses of brothers, sisters and others, the availability in the shops of high quality writing in paperback, and the need for presents at Christmas time and birthdays, will all combine to provide a peer-supported supply of books owned by children.

The poetry table can support children's increasingly informed reference to poetry in books in a number of other ways, as their reading aloud and listening at the weekly meetings becomes established. For instance, some children will expect to read the work they discover on the table to the whole class at the time when their pleasure and enjoyment is at its keenest and there are listeners available. Some children will find the confidence they have previously lacked, to read to everybody. Whichever is the case, the social origins of a response to poetry are beginning to draw upon and endorse the value of private reading.

Children may leave their personal anthologies on the poetry table to gain an informal audience. They may leave examples of their own writing, perhaps as an alternative to reading them aloud immediately to companions. A result of this is that children may read each other's work either at the weekly meetings or within day to day informal exchanges. Teachers may feed the reading culture by leaving their own books on the table, as a reader among readers. They may also leave examples of their own writing, as a writer among writers.

In these ways, and others besides, the poetry table supports those public contexts in which children may act as models for each other, to celebrate the value and process of finding poems to admire. It supports, too, the gradual progress of children's reading and composing; and encourages the development, and the acknowledgement, of an intertextuality between what they hear, read and make for themselves in writing. Finally, to summarize, the poetry table endorses the many contexts outside the classroom which are a part of children's emergent commitment to listening to poems, reading them, and composing their own.

Approaching intertextuality

The principle I want to emphasize as important to any pedagogy for teaching poetry is that children's commitment to poetry consists of patterns of symbiosis between their activities as listeners, readers, tellers and writers in various public and private contexts. Rather than being a goal to aim for, poetry is where we begin.

At the beginning, as children read privately, collect, and make their own choices and preparations for reading aloud to school companions, they invite parents and other folk at home to be listeners to poems which they already value. The same is true of poems they have written. So when a child reads a poem aloud in the weekly meeting, or in any number of informal situations in school, the accumulated endorsement of that poem, and others, by listeners at home contributes to the school reading. This endorsement influences the reader's perception of the value of what they are doing. It also influences their perceptions of the listeners, who have been similarly engaged with other listeners at home. Not only do children choose to read the poems they will read to the meeting first to individual friends and small friendship groups, but also at these times they discuss and review the participation of parents and others in their listening, reading and composing activities. Such communal knowledge is a part of the reading culture.

In such ways children begin to be interested in the explicitly aesthetic considerations of the Secondary Imagination (Auden, 1975). This they do by adopting the behaviours of the Primary Imagination, learned in their lives before school, and evident in the playground. It is a progress attended by a growing ability to engage appropriately with poems as a result of doing so together with others, in a context where individual and private response is endorsed by communal knowledge, and where they experience their own insights and pleasure in an idea expressed in a certain way, reflected in the responses and interpretations of others. A context where they begin to become conscious of the pleasurable utility of poetic form in language which, when heard in the playground, they did not even notice. Similarly, they become aware, in this instance, of their connectedness with others by recognizing what they share. In such ways reading and composing gain the same immediacy as other childhood experiences.

From using private reading as a source for reading aloud to companions, children begin to notice the effects of doing so upon their own private reading. They notice the ways in which they are also influenced by what they learn from their companions' private reading of poems and of others composing poetry. Over time they will become aware also that their private choosing of poems influences the private reading activity of their companions. Their listening will be instructed by how others listen, their reading aloud in public by companions doing the same thing. Their own writing will be 'informed' by companions' listening, public reading aloud and composition. In these ways everything they do becomes informed by a shared sub-text or a common life with poetry in the classroom.

The claim I want to make about the encouragement of children's earliest commitment to poetry from books, is that it is best achieved concurrently with an interest in the reading, composing and even listening of companions. This, because of the nature of poetry, the origins within language of our attachment to it, the nature of childhood and the relevance of Vygotsky's distinction between 'learning' and 'development'. The potential of such a coalition with a class of eight- and nine-year-olds is much the same as breakfast time with Echo!

I have tried to describe how we may anticipate children's development as effective readers and composers of poems by establishing appropriate learning contexts, where children's relationships with each other are mediated by the effects of the poetic function of language, and their responses to poems are supported by those relationships, and where it really is not too fanciful to anticipate children listening to other children listening.

If we preserve in writing the features of the special communicativeness of a reading and writing, telling and listening culture, we may notice a further instance of intertextuality which is a result of children becoming more conscious, alone and together, of the effects of poems upon them. This is a learning context where the memorable speech of poetry, as described by Auden, begins to inform the lives and the conversations of children, where ways of speaking a poem inform ways of speaking in conversation in childhood, where listening to the voices of companions telling of the effects of poems gains something of the same kind of appeal as reading a poem or being a listener to another's reading. This last instance of intertextuality is worth our most attentive listening, for it is a confirmation of the routes by which children may most easily come to value poetry in school. It is evidence of how we may succeed where previously we have not. We may hear endorsements of the principle I have been attempting to focus upon, the kind which this child offers as he describes why he wants to choose sometimes where, and when, and how, and what, to write:

> I think it is important that you shouldn't always do what you're told in writing. You ought to be allowed to write what you want. If you're told all your life to do what other people tell you, then you'll find that you won't have anything to show that's really yours.
> (Sam, aged 9)

As I mentioned earlier, the principle is, I believe, relevant to working with young teachers. Public routes to private understanding can enable them to recall these important ways of thinking with language, and the role earlier fulfilled by parents and other adults at home will now be discharged by flatmates, landladies, partners, husbands or wives. Perhaps, whatever student teachers' previous experience of poetry, as pupils, may have been, they will be losing contact with those ways, as Brodsky suggests. No doubt the pressures of the 'idiomatic' existence are increasing all the while, but language determines our connection with poetry. As young teachers set out to explore the teaching of poetry there is a real value in considering how we are all in it together.

CONCLUSION

My concern has been with beginnings, ones which may help children and teachers to connect simply with poetry, to continue to know the kinds of purposes it has within languages, and to employ them for themselves. By making choices and testing them in public ways, they may shape public statements of value which refine a commitment to further choosing. Throughout, we are asking them to know more about what they already know, though in a specifically literate way. The way begins in the community, for it depends upon language, and it is returned to the community again as children recognize shared pleasures and insist upon focusing on common values in conversation. Where it takes them in-between is for children to decide within both private and public contexts. However, it demands a pedagogy to make it possible.

My interest has been to suggest how the claim that poetry is 'lingual' is as important to our strategies for teaching poetry successfully as it is for an understanding of what poetry is. Teaching demands that we attend to all those things about people which predispose them to all language, and that includes poetry, and to informing their knowledge that poetry is poetry and not something else.

REFERENCES

Auden, W. H. (1963) Making, knowing and judging. In *The Dyer's Hand and Other Essays*. London: Faber.
Brodsky, J. (1991) Inaugural address as American Poet Laureate, 30 October, Library of Congress. Reprinted as 'Laureate of the supermarkets', in *Poetry Review*, (1992) **81** (84), pp. 4–8.
Carson, C. (1988) *The Irish for No*. Newcastle: Bloodaxe.
Geertz, C. (1983) Notions of primitive thought. In J. Miller (ed.) *States of Mind*. London: BBC Publications.
Hauge, O. (1991) *Selected Poems* (translated by Robin Fulton). New York: White Pine Press.
Hoggart, R. (1992) *An Imagined Life* (*Life and Times*, vol 3: 1959–91). London: Chatto and Windus.
Holub, M. (1992) *The Jingle Bell Principle*. Newcastle: Bloodaxe.
Jakobson, R. (1960) Closing statement: linguistics and poetics. In T. Sebeok (ed.) *Style in Language*, Cambridge, MA: MIT Press.
Langer, S. K. (1942) *Philosophy in a New Key*. Cambridge, MA: Harvard University Press.
Rosenblatt, L. (1978) *The Reader, the Text, the Poem*. Carbondale: Southern Illinois University Press.
Slobin, D. I. and Welsh, C. A. (1971) Elicited imitations as a research tool in developmental linguistics. In C. S. Lavatelli (ed.) *Language Training in Early Childhood Education*, Urbana: University of Illinois Press.
Vygotsky, L. S. (1978a) The role of play in development. In M. Cole, V. John-Steiner, S. Scribner and E. Souberman (eds), *Mind in Society,* Cambridge, MA: Harvard University Press.
Vygotsky, L. S. (1978b) Interaction between learning and development. In M. Cole, V. John-Steiner, S. Scribner and E. Souberman (eds), *Mind in Society,* Cambridge, MA: Harvard University Press.

Chapter 10

Making Sense of Poetry: Beginning Teachers Talking about Poems

Peter Millward

In this chapter I want to consider some of the contributions made by a small group of PGCE primary students as they engaged in one of the activities designed to produce data on children's constructs of poetry (described by Linda Thompson in Chapter 1). The data on which this chapter is based was gathered as part of a research project designed to produce information on children's and teachers' constructs of poetry. This data has yet to be coded and analyzed, but eventually it will be set beside data gathered from the children's activities so that we can consider the differences between the two sets and explore some of the relationships which seem to exist between teachers' and children's poetic constructs. The work with student teachers could be expected to provide a link between the two. For the present, though, I want to use the data to reflect upon the students' constructs of poetry and upon the ways in which these constructs are managed. I want to suggest that the students' knowledge about poetry is presented in ways which reveal their constructs of poetry, and that their understanding of poetry is described through their engagement in activities such as the one presented here.

Three students were asked to look at a selection of poems printed on cards. They were asked to consider each poem and to come to a group decision about which of the poems they liked best. In practice, this meant reading each poem aloud, making some comments on the poem and discarding those poems which did not appeal to any of the students. At the end of the activity, they were left with two poems which they liked ('Oh, we have to say we've got a tie for first'). They were then able to give some reasons for identifying these two poems as being the best. The activity was designed to encourage the informants to talk about poetry and to develop their understanding of poetry.

It is apparent that what I have to say in this chapter about the students' understanding of poetry is related directly to the developing context through which they are seen to be talking about the poems. The comments which they make about poetry are responses to what they were asked to do (identify the poem which they liked best). Their contributions reflect, as well, the doubts shared by the members of the group concerning what was expected of them, the tentative way in which they explored each other's knowledge and the level upon which they could agree to discuss poetry with one another. It is important to keep these points in mind. Nevertheless, it seems reasonable to make some remarks about their understanding of poetry and about the way that understanding was presented and developed.

There were two quite distinct phases in the students' management of the activity. The early part was characterized by a sense of uncertainty. The students were uncertain about the task, uncertain about what was expected of them and uncertain about the way the others would contribute. They were also uncertain about the poems: the way in which they should respond to the poems and the way in which they should talk about the poems. All of this uncertainty meant that they were not clear about the form an appropriate contribution would take. Their uncertainty was part of the context and it reflected their knowledge about poetry. Their comments on the poems, during these early stages, were of a very general nature and only rarely were they supported by reference to specific features of the poems. Towards the end of the activity, however, they were reaching towards a group decision about the poems they had read, and they presented themselves as being much more confident in the task. They also seemed to know each other better as commentators on poetry. They seemed ready to back up their statements about the poems with evidence, and their comments were much more detailed and precise. They appeared happier with the poetry and happier with the task. They reached the end of the activity when they were able to sum up what they thought about the poems. They were able to do this as they managed to find their way into the task and discover what the group was prepared to accept as appropriate contributions. Their talk about the poems was a feature of the way they managed to present the activity to themselves and to outside observers.

So, in the early stages, the students' comments on the poems were characterized by feelings of insecurity and uncertainty. They felt insecure in the task and uncertain about the poetry. They really did not know how to respond on either level. Sometimes this was revealed directly as, for instance, when one of the group pointed to her inferior knowledge about poetry:

> I just read it and think ... I'm like non-literate like that.
> I should be a bit more appreciative really.

She might have felt that this was the only way she could make a contribution to a discussion about poetry, the only way she could prepare the group for the comments she might want to make as the discussion developed. At the end of the activity, and after the group had made its decisions about the poems, this student challenged one of the others to admit to having a literary background:

> Do you do English literature?
> No.
> Did you do A-level English?
> No.
> I suppose you've done literature in Spanish.

It seems as though she wanted to attribute the difficulties she had in talking about poetry to her uncertain knowledge about poetry. She seemed to be shifting responsibility away from herself as she sought to describe the students' contributions in terms of their varied educational experiences. She certainly seemed anxious to account for the difficulties she experienced in talking about poetry:

> I did German literature at A-level which is the last time I sort of looked at anything literally and tried to decipher it.

The students' comments suggest, though, that they did not see it purely as a matter of education, for they seemed to present poetic sensibility as a reflection of upbringing:

> What does your mother specialise in?
> My mother, she's a housewife.
> Because mine specialised in English.
> So there we are.

However, even the student with the literary parent adopted a defensive attitude when she talked about poetry, and this was quite marked in the early part of the exchange. They were all prepared to acknowledge their limited knowledge about poetry, but they made it quite clear, as well, that much of their uncertainty was based on their perception of poetry as problematic and difficult. They found it difficult because poetry can be difficult, it can be difficult to appreciate and difficult to talk about. It can be a challenging form of language, and even within the selection of poems used for the children's activities, they found examples of 'the kind of poem you have to read about three times'. For these students, there was a sense in which people had to get into poems, as they had to get into activities in which they were required to talk about poems. It is evident that even as the context contributed to this sense of uncertainty about poetry during the early stages of its presentation, so, reflexively, was that context managed and described as the participants demonstrated the uncertain nature of their response to poetry.

It is interesting to see how the student teachers coped with, and presented, this sense of uncertainty. They did so, for example, as they managed to present a poetic response as a personal thing:

> It's personal, yes. What you appreciate is different to what someone else appreciates.

They went on to account for this personal response in terms of feelings:

> That's the thing about poems, you are trying to reflect what you feel.
> The poem reflects what the writer feels about poems.

They claimed that good poems 'really give you a feel of it'. They accepted that poems were 'often very personal' and that whilst poems might be 'wet and a waste of time' if looked at from one point of view, 'for the [other] person they were not'. So strongly was this sense of a personal response linked to affective rather than cognitive apprehensions, that any disagreement was seen to affect those involved at a personal level and was presented as either an apology or a rather cutting remark:

> I'm not particularly bothered by that one, personally, I'm afraid.

By treating poetic response as a personal thing, the students managed to cope with their lack of knowledge about poetry and with the problems they encountered as they bumped into the subtleties of poetic form. Of course, it is just trite to say that we respond to poetry in personal ways, but this data seems to suggest that the personal quality in poetic responses might be reinforced by teachers who do not know a lot about poetry. It is both easier and more appropriate to ask someone what a poem means to them, than to try to describe what it means and show how it achieves what it means. It is appropriate to ask, for example, 'What do you think about this poem?' or even, 'What do you feel about this poem?' It is appropriate to invite personal responses, and it is easy to shelter behind a personal response. These students were contributing appropriately and taking cover, and it worked quite well.

It seems as if this uncertainty was presented, as well, through the way in which the informants described their responses to the poems. They seemed to respond to each poem as a whole rather than to features of the poem, and they seemed to respond in a very general way. The transcript is littered with short statements describing personal, evaluative responses and nothing more:

> I don't like the poem.
> That one's quite nice, isn't it?
> I like that.
> I think it's not ... it's not ... it's not bad.
> I bet you like this one.
> Oh, I like that.

Of course, it is important to see these comments in the light of the task (identify the poem which you liked best), but they are, as well, the way the students talked about poetry and the way they were invited to talk about poetry by people who thought they knew a bit about poetry. These comments can be seen as typical responses to a poem, and they helped the students to develop the idea of a personal response and a response which was not bound about with explanations. Their contributions seem to suggest that people do not have to know much about poetry to be able to say what they do not like. In this regard, poems are like paintings, and though I may not know much about art, I know what I like. It is possible to make appropriate responses to poems without knowing much about poetry.

It is apparent from these short and sometimes immediate responses that the poems were not treated as good or bad in themselves but insofar as they were perceived to be so by the reader. The comments were personalized and the one statement (from those quoted above) which seemed to present the quality of the poem as a feature of the poem ('That one's quite nice, isn't it?') was more than just the exception which serves to prove the rule, for it was formulated in a way which brought out the speaker's uncertainty and projected her need for approval. It is evident in the responses to the poems recovered from this data, that no poem was 'either good or bad' but as 'thinking [made] it so', and it is clear that by responding in this way the students managed to produce an appropriate response (a personal response) and, at the same time, protect themselves from having to say very much about poetry and poems.

Even when they did make attempts to describe features of the poems, and they did this increasingly as the activity developed, their descriptions were only loosely linked to their evaluative judgements on the poem. From time to time, in the early part of the engagement, the students identified specific details in the poem which they considered to be worthy of comment, but there still remained a gap between their comments on features of the poem and their claim that they either liked or disliked the poem. Often their comments seemed to follow their judgements and sometimes they reached beyond these judgements:

> I like that. It has got rhyme as well.
> I like that ... and that's very simple imagery.

Sometimes the two were just put side by side and linked by association:

> I don't like that one at all, it's too overly clever.

They seemed to take care, in the early part of the discussion, not to account directly for what they felt about a poem.

These references to features of the form ('it has got rhyme as well' and 'that's very simple imagery') were not typical of the early stages of the activity. When they did try to account for their responses, these students were more inclined to do so on the basis of what the poem meant for them. They kept the personal approach to the fore and they directed their attention towards the meaning of the poem. Insofar as they related their judgements to features of the poem, they did so on the basis of content:

> I don't like that poem, don't understand what it is going on about.

Later on they were appreciative of the fact that one of the poems had a helpful title:

> Thank goodness for the title otherwise we would be completely lost.

They presented poems as problematic as they presented them as linguistic puzzles or little mysteries which had to be solved:

> Is that what it is talking about?

And they talked of deciphering poems. In the first part of the activity they chose to ignore the poetic quality in the poems and treated them, instead, as particularly challenging pieces of comprehension. They might not have known what they meant (or even to have expected to know what they meant), but they were much more ready to explore the content of the poems and they did not appear very keen to draw attention to features of the form. They were not surprised that it was difficult to decide on the meaning of a poem:

> Sometimes, I think ... because you can't get into the other person's mind you don't really understand what they are on about.

It seemed safe to focus on meaning in this way because the poet's (and the poem's) meaning remained inaccessible. Furthermore, the students frequently referred to good poems as simple poems ('I like that one because it's very simple') whilst they were much less enthusiastic about poems which could be dismissed as 'too overly clever' or 'too pretentious'. Once again, it is possible to see how the students managed their responses to the poems through the developing context. It seems that they were able to present the difficulties they had in making the poems meaningful as features of the poems, and they used these features to support their responses. People who are unsure about poetry may yet manage to produce appropriate responses to poetry as they present their contributions as uncertain, personal interpretations.

It is apparent that these students made judgements about the poems before they went on to account for their judgements. They did this over the course of the activity as they moved from immediate, evaluative responses to more thoughtful, considered accounts designed to explain their choice of good poems. They also did it with individual poems. They marked their response after the reading and then identified features of the poem which could help to explain that response. The students considered how the poems were meaningful and how they worked to affect them after they had found them to be meaningful and affecting, and it is evident that they applied their knowledge about poetry only when they had responded to the poem. It is also clear that whilst the students' knowledge about poetry may not have helped them to respond to a poem, it certainly helped them to make sense of their responses. Talking about poetry helped them to see more in poems. This might suggest something quite important about the assumption that knowledge about language helps people to be more competent and effective language users.

The feeling of uncertainty which characterized so many of the students' contributions in the early part of the activity gave way to one of greater confidence as the context was developed and as the participants came to see what counted as an appropriate contribution. It is important to appreciate this change, and that can best be done by scanning quickly across the discussion and noticing how it works as a learning engagement. It is possible to show how the participants managed the task in ways which enabled them, as the engagement developed, to consider the poems before them in more depth. Once again, it is important to appreciate the relationship between the management of the context and the exploration of the poems. This works in obvious ways, as when poems were discarded and the focus was sharpened until the students were looking only at their two favourite poems; but it works, as well, in ways that are much more subtle and pervasive. As the students came to see more in the poems, the context was developed (from, say, a reading of poems with appropriate but immediate and general responses to a discussion about poetry supported by examples from specific poems) and as the context was developed the students came to see more in the poems. This reflexive force is very powerful.

It is quite interesting to trace what happened. At the start of the activity, the students responded in a tentative way and they were concerned to demonstrate their support for one another:

> I quite liked that one.
> Yes, I liked that one.

The students' responses were immediate and undemanding, and they offered no information to explain, or account for, these responses. They seemed to be testing the context: trying out what might count as an appropriate response and finding out what they could say about poetry. It is clear that they treated poems as 'difficult' and 'problematic', and that they doubted their knowledge about poetry and their ability to appreciate poems properly. Already it is apparent from the data that they treated poems as being 'about something' and that they felt their difficulties arose, in part, because they could not understand what a particular poem was about. They liked a poem insofar as they were able to describe what was going on in it, and they linked their understanding to the power of a poem to present 'pictures' of this kind. A significant development occurred when the students related a particular poem ('Windy Nights') to other poetic experiences:

> So a man's a wind. I'd read this poem that was really good … was the other way round, wind was seen as a dirty old man that blew up women's skirts.

The emphasis was still on what the poem was about (the poem treated as a story), but the student was also relating the content of the poem to features of poetic form and the treatment, as she saw it, of the man as a wind. She was talking about poetry but she was not using formal metalinguistic terms. As the students turned their attention to features of the poems, they took the opportunity to explain their responses and this explanation encouraged them to consider features of the structure of the poem ('it is overly pretentious' and 'it has got rhyme as well'). They also considered their responses in terms of their professional concerns:

> Maybe it appeals to us because we are infant teachers and we know they like things that rhyme.

Furthermore, as they talked about the poems, they drew upon their knowledge of an appropriate metalanguage. Whereas before they had simply drawn attention to what was happening in the poem ('So a man's a wind'), they now talked of imagery:

> And that's very simple imagery. I like 'The soldier on the skyline fires the golden gun'.

The focus on the images created in the poem ('the way you can sort of just picture the sun coming up') is reflected in their responses ('gorgeous' and 'brilliant'), and it was clearly important to them that good poems could conjure up visual images. This was developed very vividly a little later as one of the group asked the others for help:

'The sunbeams look at you and scream'. Why is that?

And the answer was presented in visual terms:

Because the sun shines through the web. Picture the spider's web with the sun shining through it.

Though this might not have served to provide a complete explanation ('I don't know why they scream'), it did seem to satisfy the others and it enabled them to consider it a good poem because 'you can imagine it'. They were still describing personal responses to particular poems as they drew attention to the imaginative quality in their responses, but they were also supporting these responses as they described what they saw in the poems. They were still carefully guarding and protecting their knowledge about poetry, for all you can do with images is share them. They shared the 'pictures' which the poems evoked for them and their descriptions could not be challenged.

The discussion shifted away from specific examples and the participants used their experience of a particular poem to talk about poetry in general. They did this as they considered what annoyed them in one of the poems which, in any case, was 'not really a poem' but 'just a paragraph ... [put] into verses'. It led them to consider sonnets ('usually a bit wet') and to think that the poet must have been thinking 'about bad poems rather than good poems ... because there [was] no rhyming in it'. It is clear that they were working to justify their responses to the poems and they were doing this in terms of the form of the poem as well as the meaning. They had been pushed in this direction by the poem ('A Good Poem') and, though they did not think it a good poem, it is possible to see that they appreciated there was more to a poem than what it appeared to mean and more to a poem than verses and rhymes. There is something special about a poem, and the next poem ('Spider') was disappointing because it was:

the sort of poem you can write yourself and therefore it's not anything particularly special.

Even as they struggled to express their own responses ('I think ... it's not, it's not bad' and 'I think it's quite good'), and even as they wondered whether it might have been written by a child, they began to appreciate the implications of this personal approach. The uncertainty with which they were accounting for their responses and the personal quality of their accounts started to worry them. One of the three students directed a question to the others:

How do you tell a good poem from a bad poem?

It was a significant moment and, for the first time, they were obliged to focus on features of the poem. They had to call upon, and display, their knowledge about poetry. Although they tried to evade the question by referring to personal responses, they were made to think that more was required of them:

You can still tell a good poem [from] a bad poem ... to a certain extent, can't you?

They were unhappy ('What do you mean?'), and they were given an example:

> Like good use of language ... like not using 'nice' all the time.

And because they still would not respond, they were encouraged to consider the professional implications:

> I mean like ... if you've got your class to write poems, how do you like get them to be better?

It is not easy to say why one poem is better than another, and they fell back on examples and trusted that the others would understand:

> I really like him [Robert Frost]. You know what I mean.

And everyone did know what she meant because they were supportive and because they wanted to sustain the context and because it was considered acceptable to go only so far when talking about poetic responses. They were still reluctant to say much about poetry and so they had another poem to fill the gap.

This poem was challenging and they responded by presenting the puzzling quality in the poem ('Why Puss?') and, as they attempted to account for the poet's choice of words, they showed that they treated poems as explicable even though, as in this case, it may be difficult to 'get into the other person's mind' and even though it is not always possible to 'really understand what they are on about'. It is clear that they were upset by poems which appeared to them to be deliberately and gratuitously opaque. This approach offered them another helpful 'getting by' strategy, and by adopting this kind of attitude they managed to keep their knowledge about poetry unthreatened whilst preserving the 'puzzling' quality in poems. We ought to acknowledge that that is an easy (and reasonable) criticism to level at a poem which we do not understand.

When they came to read the last poem ('Overhead on a Saltmarsh'), they seemed to come together as a group and they seemed able to share their enthusiasm for their favourite poems. They responded immediately and upon impulse, and they linked their approval of the poem to the way in which it was read ('Very well read, Kesta'). They expressed their excitement, and thus they emphasized the personal quality of their responses. However, they did not leave it there, but immediately accounted for their excitement by presenting quotations from the poems. The focus was on images and the thoughts engendered by the poem, and their recognition of the personal quality in all poetic responses was still apparent. They accounted for their responses by saying what they thought, rather than what they knew. This preserved the sense of uncertainty and the sense of mystery in poems. It also provided the personal touch:

> What are you thinking?
>
> I thought it was, as you said, a tree.
>
> I thought it was a tree.
>
> I think I thought Saltmarsh and thought pond for some reason.

They were reaching towards shared agreement about personal perceptions, and their language was a feature of the context as surely as it was typical of poetry talk.

The reading of the last poem seemed to inspire them. They talked confidently about the poem and they contributed with confidence to the activity. Their enthusiasm and confidence was apparent as they were happy to account for what they liked:

I liked that one because it's more fantasy and I like fantasy.

I liked that one because it is very simple ... more down to earth and that's the kind of person I am.

I like this 'Early in the Morning' one because it makes me think of that of scenery which gives me a good feeling.

I like the mystery.

You can imagine it can't you? Misty pond area, and goblin and nymph counting its beads.

This one's got rhyme in it and I think that's the reason I like it.

And I like that because it's a mixture of a conversation but it is poetry and it rhymes.

I like the structure of that.

I think this is really clever, but this one is really clever as well.

I like the bit where it goes ... 'and over the back of the chimney stack explodes the silent sun'.

Their personal responses were linked to their knowledge about poetry. To the very end they were concerned to present their responses as personal, but they were now prepared to explain these responses. They did so in terms of specific features of poetic experience: imagery, feelings, structure, fantasy. They seemed to be taking much less account of the content of the poem. It seems that having found these poems accessible (through the images they invoke) they could now see how they were effective. They were able to account for their responses in poetic terms.

Of course, these comments referred to the two poems which they liked the best, and they liked them because they were accessible. Once the students' interest had been captured by the poems, they were able to identify features of the poems which they liked and this, of course, enabled them to talk about the poems. In talking about the poems they shared knowledge about poetry and they showed each other what counted as an appropriate contribution to a discussion on poetry. It certainly seems that knowledge about poetry can only be applied when people have responded to poetry. Initially, the students seemed to be drawn by the images in the poems and the 'pictures' the poems presented. They could, of course, have been attracted by the rhythms or the rhyme patterns. However, it seems that any poem which did not affect them was dismissed not as formless but as meaningless. All they could do when confronted with such a poem was to try to puzzle out what it meant. This was unlikely to lead them to consider its poetic qualities and, indeed, it may have prevented them from even treating it as poetic (except insofar as they could present it as enigmatic). Clearly, focusing on what a poem means can be distracting but without a sense of meaningfulness it is not easy to be affected by a poem.

When people are confronted with a poem their first concern, as with any act involving language, is to produce a response. It is quite appropriate for a response to a poem to be evaluative. It is also expected that the response will be of a personal nature. The students' response was related to the extent to which they found the poems meaningful and that seemed to be linked to the power of the poem to evoke images. For language to work, people have to assume that contributions, written or aural, are produced in good faith and are produced to be meaningful. This natural and necessary assumption, which everyone engaged in using language applies, served to direct the attention of the students to the meaning of the poems. People make language meaningful, and only when they find it meaningful can they go on to account for the ways in which it is meaningful. It is only when the students began to understand (or feel) that a poem might have something to say to them that they started to look at the ways in which the poem was effective. They accepted that poems are difficult, but they were not prepared to spend much time seeking out the meaning of particular poems (probably because of the nature of the task) and those which did not touch them immediately were likely to be dismissed as too complex or overly pretentious. They began to explain their responses when they came across a poem which made sense to them and their initial explanations were in terms of what the poem meant to them. For these students, it was the power of the images, the 'pictures which the poems create', which they drew upon to account for their positive responses. These images provided the link between the meaning of the poem and the poetic form in which this language was presented. They were now able to talk about their responses, to talk about the way the poems were made meaningful and about the ways in which the poems affected them. As they talked about the poems, they attended to the poetic quality in the poems. They moved away from thinking about what a poem means to consider how the poem works and that led them into talking about poetic genre and poetic structure.

It is clear that people have to talk about poetry if they are to be able to say more than what they like and dislike. Poetry might be a very personal thing, but it is understood in conversations and discussions such as these. People have to be able to share their personal responses and relate their responses to the poems. If they cannot do this, there is nothing to be said or done. These students were sharing their experiences of the poems as they helped each other to understand what they liked. To do this they had to describe their personal responses in terms of the poems and they had to find a language to talk about poetry. They also had to manage their contributions to the activity. All of these things take some time.

Name Index

Akyer, Ayse 53
Andersen, Benny xiv, 30, 35, 36
Andresen, Ute 14, 21
Anscombe, G.E.M. 43
Arnold, Matthew 26
Artaud, Antonin 17
Atkinson, J. 37, 43
Auden, W.H. 82–3, 84

Ball, Hugo 16, 21
Baudelaire, Charles 56, 58–62
Bell, R. 1, 11, 43, 54
Benton, Peter 44, 51–3, 54
Benton, Michael 1, 11, 24, 28, 38–9, 42–3, 51, 54
Bolt, S. 25, 28
Bradley, L. 27, 28
Brecht, Bertolt 13, 16
Brierley, J. 26, 28
Brodsky, J. xiii, 77, 79, 83, 84
Brownjohn, Sandy 52, 54
Brumfit, C. 53
Bryant, P. 27, 28
Buchbinder, D. 40, 43
Burssens, Gaston 65, 68
Busch, Wilhelm 16
Busta, Christine 13
Byram, Mike xi

Calthrop, K. 28
Calvino, Italo 20
Carroll, Lewis 19
Carson, Ciaran 77, 84
Carter, R. 2, 4–7, 11, 53
Chambers, Gary 53
Chomsky, Noam 15
Chukovsky, K. 26, 28
Clare, John 25
Clarke, D. 53
Cole, M. 84
Collie, Joanne 52–3, 54

Constable, H. 11
Constantine, D. 53

Damsma, Harm 64, 76
de la Mare, Walter 24, 28
de Moor, Willem vii, xiii, 63
Dias, P. 38, 40, 43
Dickinson, Emily xiv, 30, 36
Donne, John 40
Doyle, C. 41, 43
Duff, A. 52–3, 54

Ede, J. 28
Ehmcke, Susanne 20
Eliot, T.S. 40
Enzensberger, Hans Magnus 12

Farrow, S. 11
Fleming, Mike vii, xi, xii, 43
Fournier, Jean-Marie vii, xii
Fox, G. 24, 28
Frost, Robert 92
Fulton, Robin 84

Garbe, Burckhard 13
Gard, R. 25, 28
Geertz, C. 79, 84
Gelberg, Hans-Joachim 13
Glaser, B. 11
Guggenmos, Josef 13

Hacks, Peter 13
Hall, Linda vii, xii, 11, 22
Hansson, Gunnar 68, 70, 76
Hardy, Thomas 38
Hauge, Olav 80, 84
Hayhoe, M. 38, 40, 43, 47, 52, 54
Heaney, Seamus 39
Hermann, Gisela 47, 54
Hill, J. 53

Hoggart, R. 77, 84
Holland, Norman 70, 76
Holub, Miroslav 79, 84
Hughes, Ted 40
Hunfield, Hans 46, 52–3, 54
Hurst, K. 1, 11, 43, 54

Iser, Wolfgang 38, 68, 70, 76

Jakobson, R. 79, 84
Jandl, Ernst 16
Jensen, Thorkild Borup vii, xii
Jesperson, Otto ix
Johnson, Thomas H. xiv, 36
John-Steiner, V. 84
Jones, A. 53
Joyce, James 17

Kirchner, Athanasius 18
Knauth, Alfons 52, 54
Kristeva, Julia 12, 17, 21
Krüss, James 13

Langer, S.K. 79, 84
Larsson, R. 41, 43
Lavatelli, C.S. 84
Lear, Edward 16, 20
Legutke, Michael 45–53, 54
Leiris, Michel 19
Levin, S. 1, 11
Long, M. 53
Lullus, Raymundus 18

McGough, Roger 42
Maley, A. 52–3, 54
Mallarmé, Stéphane 18
Manz, Hans 13
Mattenklott, Gundel vii, 12, 14, 21
Mayröcker, Friederike 17, 21
Merrick, B. 37, 43
Meyer, Herman 19, 21
Miller, J. 84
Millward, Peter viii, xi, xiii, 11, 85
Milne, A.A. 27, 28
Morgan, Carol viii, xiii
Mörike, E.F. 19
Moulding, S. 53
Mummert, Ingrid 46–7, 54
Murray, D. 40, 43

Nash, W. 2, 4–7, 11
Neruda, Pablo 53
Norton, J. 11

Parker, S. 47, 52, 54
Peirce, Charles S. 61

Perec, Georges 16, 20
Pirrie, Jill 45–51, 54
Poe, Edgar Allen 70
Poole, Brian 12
Prévert, Jacques 45, 46, 51, 53
Purves, Alan C. 64

Queneau, Raymond 20

Rabelais, François 17
Reeves, J. 37, 43
Richards, I.A. 38, 43
Rosen, Michael 45–6, 53, 54
Rosenblatt, L. 38, 80, 84
Roubaud, Jacques 20
Roussel, Raymond 19
Rühmkorf, Peter 19, 21
Sansom, Clive 25, 29
Scannell, Vernon 28, 29, 38
Scribner, S. 84
Sebeok, T. 84
Shakespeare, William 26, 40
Sidaway, S. 37, 43
Slater, Stephen 52–3, 54
Slobin, D.I. 80, 84
Sola Pinto, V. da 29
Souberman, E. 84
Spears, M.K. 41, 43
Steiner, G. 38–41, 43
Strauss, A. 11
Strong, L.A.G. 26, 29

Tarleton, R. 51, 54
Taylor, Alexander xiv, 35
Teasey, J. 1, 11, 43, 54
Ten Brinke, Steven 64
Terrell, C.F. 43
Thompson, Linda viii, xi, 11, 85
Touponce, W. 1, 11, 38, 43

van Ostaijen, Paul 68–71, 76
Vygotsky, L.S. 79–80, 83, 84

Wade, B. 37, 43
Wain, J. 41, 43
Walter, Colin viii, xiii, 77
Welsh, C.A. 80, 84
Whitton, K. 53
Williams, William Carlos xiv, 41, 43
Witkin, Robert 64
Wittgenstein, L. 40, 43
Wood, J. 39, 43
Wood, L. 39, 43
Wordsworth, William 26

Yates, W.B. 38

Subject Index

activities in class xiii, 17, 23, 25, 31–6, 45–51
aesthetics 1, 4, 6, 17, 18, 20, 37, 39, 47, 51, 55, 68, 70, 82
affective element 7–8
alliteration 13, 27
alphabet games 16–18
anthologies 13, 32, 64
art xii, xiii, 25, 51–2, 77
attitudes towards poetry:
    pupils' xi, xii; *see also* awareness; difficulty; dislike; experience
    teachers' xi, 22, 30, 37, 55, 64, 78, 85–94
audio recording *see* tape-recording
aural quality of poetry 3–6, 10, 28
author's text 65–9, 72, 76
awareness of poetic genre 2–3, 5–7, 9–10

babies' experience of poetry 12–13, 17, 79
baccalauréat examination xii, 55, 62
ballads 33, 34
Bullock Report 22, 23

characteristic features of poetry 8–10, 15, 33–4, 41–2, 57, 90, 94
children's poetry 13, 20, 32, 80
classroom activities *see* activities
comprehension exercises 25, 39, 89
computers *see* information technology
confidence, teachers' xi; *see also* attitudes
constructs of poetic genre 1, 7, 9, 85
contingent difficulties 37, 41
contouring of language 2–3, 5–6, 28
creativity xii, 7, 23, 25, 35, 40, 45
critical awareness 6
curiosity, pupils' 30, 31, 35
curriculum xi, xii, 1, 2, 10, 24. 26–8, 42, 63, 66, 77, 78; *see also* National Curriculum

dance 25
Denmark xi, xii, 30
'difficulty' with poetry xii, 1, 30, 37–42, 86–7, 89–90, 94

dislike of poetry xii, 13, 22, 37, 39, 53, 64
drama xii, 13, 25, 42, 56, 64, 66
drawing pictures 71–6; *see also* art
Durham Poetry Project xii
Durham Poetry Symposium xi, 64
Dutch Anthology Project 64
dyslexia 27

Education Reform Act 1
emotional content of poetry 25–6, 39
English language, teaching of 1, 9
    as a foreign language xiii, 46
enjoyment xii, 22, 28, 31, 34, 37, 53, 69, 78, 80–1, 84
ethnocentricity xii, 47
examinations 22, 39, 42, 55; *see also* baccalauréat
experience of poetry
    babies' 12–13, 17, 79
    children's 7–8, 31, 34
    teachers' 85–94
experiencing poetry xii, 31–7, 42, 64–76

figurative language 18–19, 34, 36, 41; *see also* imagery; metaphor
Fleurs du mal (Baudelaire) 56–62
foreign language teaching xiii, 45–53
France xi, xii, 14, 20, 45, 55–62
free verse 23, 27
French National Institute of Pedagogical Research (NRP) xii, 55, 56

games with language xii, 12–20, 69, 79
Germany xi, 13, 14, 17, 19, 45, 52, 63
given knowledge 7–8, 10
grammar 2, 15, 52; *see also* syntax
group interaction xiii, 2, 19, 25, 31–5, 37, 42, 52, 71–6, 79–94; *see also* activities in class

Half Our Future 22
heightened language 45–6; *see also* figurative language
historical associations 37
HMI 24, 26

imagery 91, 93–4; *see also* metaphor
information technology 51
intertextuality 82–4
intuitive knowledge 7–8, 10

jingles xii, 12, 31, 34, 42

KAL teaching 1
Kingman Report 1, 9

labyrinths of letters 18
language
    contouring 2–3, 5–6, 28
    poetic nature xiii
    teaching xi, xiii, 1, 9, 32, 46, 51–2
    use of 2, 6, 14–15, 26; *see also* speech
    see also metalanguage
Language in Education Group xi
Language Performance in Schools 22
learning difficulties 27
lexical choice 2, 3, 5, 6, 37, 39; *see also* vocabulary
limericks 20
linguistic repertoire of children 9–10
listening to poetry 31–3, 82–3
literacy, standards of 1
lullabies 12
lyrics *see* songs

Mammouth Law 63
Melopee method 65
'Melopee' (poem) 68–76
metalanguage 1, 4, 7–10, 90
metaphor xii, 1, 18, 19, 28, 41, 79; *see also* imagery
metre 28, 34
modal difficulties 38, 41
modernism 39–40
music xii, 13, 17, 31, 33, 51–2, 77; *see also* songs

National Curriculum xii, 45, 46, 77
Netherlands xi, 63–76
NRP *see* French National Institute of Pedagogical Research
nursery rhymes 7, 8, 10, 12, 27, 31, 81

ontogenetic approach xiii, 79–80
ontological difficulties 39–40

patterning of text 2, 4, 6
Pavlovian model 23
pedagogy 10, 13, 42, 77–80, 82, 84
perceptions of poetry, pupils' xiii, 1, 2, 7, 24, 37, 51, 82
personal nature of response to poetry 87–94
phonology 27
phylogenetic approach 79–80
physical movement 33
pictorial elements 51; *see also* visual impact
pidgin-dialects 15

play *see* games with language
pleasure from poetry *see* enjoyment
poem of the day 32
poetic function 79
poetry table 81–2
poets reading their own work 33
private reading 80–3
project work 22–4, 26, 32, 57
punctuation 6, 36

quotations 9, 92

rapping xii, 42
reader's text 65–8, 70, 76
reader-response 64
readers' logs 64, 66
reading, teaching of xiii, 27, 28
reading aloud *see* recitation
recitation 4–5, 25–7, 31–2, 42, 81–3, 85
reflectivity 64
response to poetry 25–6, 71–2, 77, 81–3, 86–94
rhyme xii, 3, 4–5, 7–8, 12, 15, 16, 19–20, 23, 25–8, 31, 34, 37, 51, 71, 79, 88, 90, 91, 93
rhythm 5–7, 12–13, 25, 28, 31, 33, 34, 37, 70, 93

self-expression 46, 51
shared experience *see* group interaction
simile 1, 28
songs xii, 7, 8, 10, 13, 31, 34, 42, 45, 79
sonnets 20, 91
sound patterns 2, 5, 12, 15, 27–8, 70
speech, different modes xii, 1–2, 4, 45, 83
speech patterns 12
spelling, teaching 27
spoken word *see* speech
stimulus and response 23
story telling 16, 27, 36
student's text 70–2
syntax 2, 6, 15, 37, 41, 80; *see also* grammar

tape-recording 2, 31–4, 72
teacher education xi, xiii, 13–14, 24, 78–80, 83
teacher's text 70, 72, 76
test scores 27
titles of poems 35, 89
topic-based learning 22–4, 26, 32, 57
traditional teaching methods 65

United States 63, 65
utilitarianism 23–5, 28

visual impact of poems 2–3, 17, 42, 51, 52
vocabulary 19, 26, 41, 51, 52; *see also* lexical choice

writing of poetry by children 3, 6, 14, 20, 23–5, 35, 45–53. 80–3, 91–2

Young Writers Competition 45, 47